Rescuing Sprite

Mark R. Levin

Rescuing Sprite

*A Dog Lover's Story
of Joy and Anguish*

Doubleday Large Print
Home Library Edition

POCKET BOOKS

New York London Toronto Sydney

This Large Print Edition, prepared especially for Doubleday Large Print Home Library, contains the complete, unabridged text of the original Publisher's Edition.

Pocket Books
A Division of Simon & Schuster, Inc.
1230 Avenue of the Americas
New York, NY 10020

Copyright © 2007 by Mark R. Levin

All photos courtesy of Mark R. Levin.

POCKET and colophon are registered trademarks of
Simon & Schuster, Inc.

Manufactured in the United States of America

ISBN-13: 978-0-7394-9065-5

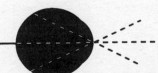

**This Large Print Book carries the
Seal of Approval of N.A.V.H.**

This book is dedicated to
my dogs,
your dogs,
and all dogs
who desperately need a home

Contents

Introduction

Who would have thought I'd write a book about a dog named Sprite? Well, actually, about a dog named Pepsi, too, and another one named Griffen.

Every dog lover has a dog story. This is mine.

For most of my life, my passions have involved big goals and big thoughts. I've spent my career as a lawyer and broadcaster working on constitutional issues, writing about public policy, and talking about current events. I've served at the highest levels of our government, and I've even written a book about the Supreme Court. So why write *this* book? Because I am, first and foremost, a dog lover. Few things in life have given me the kind of joy and, frankly, sorrow, as my relationships with my dogs. And this is especially so with an older dog we rescued from a local shelter. We called him Sprite.

Sprite was found one day roaming the streets of Silver Spring, Maryland. We believe he lost his original family—or they lost him. He was taken to a local shelter and later handed over to foster parents while awaiting a family to adopt him. We were lucky to be that family.

Sprite was so beautiful. He had big brown eyes and the softest fur I'd ever touched. As we soon learned, Sprite also suffered from serious and ultimately debilitating health problems, but he never let any of it get him down. Despite life's curveballs, he was a dignified, graceful, and courageous dog. He was friendly to all, humans and canines alike.

Sprite touched me in ways I could never have expected. He taught me to better appreciate the simple and more important things in life. He quickly became an irreplaceable member of our family and a fixture in the neighborhood. Even with all his setbacks, Sprite was full of life. He appreciated life. He cherished every moment, seeming to understand that his time left on earth would be too brief.

I loved this dog. Writing this book was both painful and cathartic for me. Reading it may be emotional for you. I hope it brings you some smiles. I know it will bring you some tears. I hope, when you're done, that you are moved to hold your dog closer in your arms—or in your memories.

ONE

Let's Call Him Pepsi

1966

I have always loved dogs. I love to look at them, to be around them, and to play with them. We grew up with dogs. When I was eight, my parents bought a puppy from a friend of a relative. He was a mixed breed, mostly black, with a little white on his chest. We named him Prince.

I remember the first time I walked Prince. He was nine weeks old or so. I put the leash around his neck and at first he wouldn't budge. I had to drag him for a bit until he (and I) got the hang of it. It didn't take him long. And he also was housetrained in no time. Prince was a very sharp dog. He brought great pleasure to the family. His only vice, if you want to call it that, was his occasional desire to run free. And when he had the urge, nothing could stop him. He'd sprint through the front door no matter how narrow the opening. He might return in a few hours, or the next day. It upset us to no end when it would happen. We were very lucky he always returned home.

Not long after we got Prince, another dog came into our family—along with a grandfather. I was taking my piano lesson when my teacher and I were interrupted by a tall man who had swaggered into the house. He was wearing a Stetson and a long leather coat. I thought he was John Wayne. My mother, Norma, said to me, "This is your grandfather, Moe." He was my mother's father, but I'd never met him before. In fact, up to that point, I don't remember anyone saying much about him. My grandmother Rose had divorced him many years earlier. He had been estranged from the family for some time. I would later learn that Pop-Pop Moe, as we called him, had served in the Marines during World War II, where he fought at Iwo Jima and Guam. The war took a toll on him. He suffered a nervous disorder that had taken most of his voice, and he strained to talk. But as I later learned, he was a lot of fun. He took my brothers and me to our first pro-wrestling match, and he took us to the racetrack, where he placed some bets for us.

On that first day he walked over to the piano, reached into his coat pocket, and pulled out a tiny Chihuahua. She was mostly black and brown with a little white. I'd never seen anything like her. My mother named her Lady Duchess of Hawthorne. Lady would be the first of three Chihuahuas in the Levin household, all of whom were closest to my mother. A few years later, Lady died from a tragic accident. As my grandfather was getting out of his car, Lady unexpectedly jumped out of the car as Pop-Pop Moe was shutting the door. Her injury was fatal, and we were all devastated, especially my mother and grandfather.

Not long thereafter we got another Lady, my favorite of the three Chihuahuas. She wasn't your typical Chihuahua. She was less yappy. She was always a puppy to me, even as she got older.

Prince welcomed the Chihuahuas into the family. He was a happy-go-lucky dog. Even when the first Lady would growl or nip at him, he thought nothing of it. Prince could have crushed any one of them in his jaws, but he'd just walk away.

Prince added so much life and joy to our family. My two brothers and I grew up with him, from elementary school through college. I will always love him, and I will never forget him. The third Lady, who we didn't own during Prince's life, died in 2000. I didn't know her as well, but I suspect she was my mother's favorite. She lived for fifteen years.

September 1998

I didn't want to deny our kids the wonderful opportunity of growing up with a dog. My wife, Kendall, wasn't so keen on the idea. She grew up with two "outside" dogs: Hobo I and Hobo II. She loved her Hobos, of course, but living with an "inside" dog is a different experience. I spent a year or so wearing Kendall down, with assistance from my two kids.

There was a storefront pet shop called Just Pets not too far from our home. For months I'd walk by the window fairly frequently to see if any of the puppies caught my eye. I wasn't sure what I was looking for, only that I'd know it when I saw it. And one day, that's exactly what happened. There he was, playing in the window. A little black pup with a white left paw and a white chest. He was the runt of the litter of six puppies and the only male. He reminded me of my beloved Prince. From the moment I saw him, I knew he was mine.

I went into the pet shop. The sign on the window said the dogs were half-border collie and half-cocker spaniel. They were asking $225. I picked him up out of the window display, held him to my chest, scratched him with one finger, and inhaled that beautiful odor of an eight- or nine-week-old puppy. After five minutes I turned to the shop owner and told him, "I want this dog." He said he could hold him for twenty-four hours. I put down a deposit, told the gentleman I'd be back with the family, and on the way out the door said to him, "Now, don't sell this dog." He said, "Don't worry, mister. I won't." I then headed straight home.

It was 1998. My daughter, Lauren, was ten years old and my son, Chase, was seven. The time was right.

As long as I can remember, Lauren has been innately sensitive to other people's feelings. She's genuinely caring and thoughtful. Lauren's face falls naturally into a smile. And she mostly sees the good in others. Lauren is a perfect companion for a dog.

Chase has always adored animals. He has no apprehension around them and they bring out his playful personality. He bonds with them immediately. Animals sense the sincerity of Chase's affection and his complete lack of reserve. They love his company.

I described the dog to Kendall and the kids. Lauren and Chase could barely contain themselves. And Kendall was excited, too. Rather than wait until the next day, we decided to go to the pet shop before it closed. Kendall invited our neighbor, Linda Levy, to come along. Linda owned a black Lab named Honey Bunch, who was six or seven years old, a gentle and mature dog.

Linda seemed to have a special knowledge about dogs. I figured it couldn't hurt. I just wanted the dog. So we piled into the car and headed for the pet shop.

Everyone oohed and ahhed over the puppy. The kids couldn't handle him enough. I could see that Kendall was smitten, as well. Linda suggested that we place the puppy on his back and see how he would react. She said that if he struggled a lot, chances are the dog would be hyperactive. So we put him on his back and he didn't do anything. He passed the test, although it really didn't make any difference to me. I paid the balance of the bill, signed various papers, collected the medical information, and we took him home.

What were we going to name this dog? Kendall liked Jet. Lauren and I liked Sporty, which had been the name of a dog my grandmother Rose owned years ago. There was Oreo and Coke. But Lauren came up with Pepsi because, she said, he was dark like the soda. Chase also liked it. Well, that was good enough for me, so he became Pepsi.

For the first few weeks, we kept Pepsi in a crate in our basement when it was time to go to sleep. This helped house-train him. For a while I slept on the sofa right next to the crate. Every time he made a noise as if he needed to go to the bathroom, I'd jump up and run him outside. And every time he did his business outside, I heaped praise on him. In no time at all, Pepsi was house-trained.

During those nights and early mornings, I spent a lot of time bonding with Pepsi. I played with him, let him rest on my chest, and had long conversations with him. I knew he was special. I could tell from the movement of his eyes, ears, and head in response to my voice that he was exceptionally intelligent. He was able to quickly pick up words and commands.

During his first year, the border collie part of Pepsi's personality took over. It caused him to race around the house, chew on furniture and clothing, and even nip the kids now and then—especially Chase. Since Chase was still quite young, it was as if Pepsi considered him part of the litter. Besides, if Pepsi didn't have sheep to herd, kids were the next best thing. When neighbors came to the door, and Pepsi was in one of his mischievous moods, we'd have to apologize for his behavior. We used to tell them, "He really is a good dog. He's just a little excited."

Frankly, I wondered to myself, When is he going to grow out of this?

One day, when he was around a year old, Pepsi's wildness stopped cold. He still had lots of energy, got into the pantry and trash now and again, and liked to sprint around the house when he was happy, but there was no more gnawing or nipping.

Pepsi was also lucky to have a wonderful friend in the neighborhood. Linda's dog, Honey Bunch, was like a big sister to Pepsi. She wasn't in the best shape, but when she saw Pepsi, her tail would wag with joy. And Pepsi loved her. He was always thrilled to see her. I believe that relationship, early in Pepsi's life, taught him to be tolerant and friendly to other dogs.

This would become crystal clear to me six years later when we adopted our second dog, Sprite.

I've never liked exercising, but I always like walking Pepsi. I walk him every morning and night, but the weekends are the best. I walk him several times around the neighborhood and we greet everyone we see. We also learn a lot about our neighbors—which kids are heading to college, who just had an operation, which family is moving—the usual stuff. Sometimes we cross the busiest street where there are several baseball and soccer fields. I check out the games while Pepsi checks out the kids. We have a good time and, for the most part, our walks are uneventful.

But there was one occasion when fate put Pepsi and me in the right place at the right time. I decided to take Pepsi on a different route, and we turned right on a road where we normally would turn left. We walked to a heavily traveled intersection. Then I saw a young girl running and screaming. It was Fran, a friend and schoolmate of Lauren's. She was holding her poodle, Dusty, in her arms. She cried out that someone had run over Dusty and drove off without stopping. The dog was in extreme pain, yipping and struggling. Fran, who was about twelve years old, was having difficulty holding him.

I held Pepsi's leash with one hand and took Dusty from Fran with the other. As I put him under my arm, I could see the problem: his front right leg was broken clear in half and was hanging by the skin. I cringe at the sight of someone else's blood or bad injuries like this, but I managed to put all of that out of my head and held him tightly so he wouldn't fall. I knew if he got to the ground, he'd do even more damage to himself.

Dusty kept struggling. It didn't take long for my arm to start aching. I needed to find someone to take Pepsi so I could hold Dusty with both arms. Thankfully, I saw a teenage neighbor, Garrett, down the street and called to him. He knew who I was and where I lived and took Pepsi home.

In the meantime, I needed to get Fran and Dusty to their home, which wasn't very far. We needed to get help—and fast (this was before cell phones were generally available).

A car with a young couple drove up to us. The guy jumped out of the car and asked me if the dog was okay. Fran told me it was the car that had hit her dog. I couldn't believe it. I guess after leaving the scene of the accident ten minutes earlier, they decided they'd better return. It was obvious to me that they were more concerned about being reported to the police for a hit-and-run than helping Fran and her severely injured dog.

I told him, "Get the hell out of here. We don't need your help now." And that's what they did. I wanted nothing to do with such heartless jerks. I had to get Dusty to a vet.

I banged on Fran's front door. Her grandmother answered. She didn't speak English and Fran's father wasn't home. I called out to Fran's mother, who I knew in passing. She ran to the door. When she saw Dusty's condition, she became nearly hysterical. Who could blame her? I told her in a stem voice, "You need to get ahold of yourself. We need to get your dog some help."

I called 911. The operator said there was nothing they could do. I asked, "Well, who do I call?" "You can call a veterinary hospital," she answered. Boy, that was helpful. I turned to Fran's mom and said, "Grab your keys. You need to drive us to the closest vet." Although no more than fifteen minutes had passed since I first came upon Fran and Dusty, the dog was suffering and my arms were becoming numb. I had to hold him in the same position to ensure that no more damage would be done to his leg.

It seemed like we were hitting every red light. Fran was in the backseat, her mom was driving, and I was sitting in the front passenger seat holding Dusty tightly. It took twenty minutes to get to the veterinary hospital. I'd never been there before, but I'd passed it many times on my way to work.

I jumped out of the car with the dog, hustled through the door, and rushed up to the receptionist. "I need help. The dog was hit by a car and his leg is nearly severed." The receptionist said, "We're closing and the vet has already gone." "You have to be kidding," I said. "Do you have a technician who can help us?"

A technician appeared. She looked at us from a distance. "The vet is gone and his condition is too severe for me to handle." This was an animal hospital! I was appalled by their heartlessness. These are people who are around animals all day. "You mean to tell me that you can't even sedate the dog so I can get him to another vet?" I asked. "We can't help you, sir." I looked at them with disgust and stormed out the door.

I got back in the car. "Okay," I said, "let's go to Pepsi's vet." Fifteen minutes later, we arrived at the Clocktower Veterinary Hospital. I was exhausted. I could barely move my arms, and I was in a cold sweat from the exertion. I wasn't in the best shape—I'm still not. I prayed the hospital was open, as it was now getting late.

We received a completely different reception from that at the other hospital. The technicians moved quickly. They took Dusty from me, immediately sedated him, and began making a splint for his leg. They said Dusty needed surgery, which required a specialist. They assured me they would stabilize him and prep him for yet another trip to another town. By now Fran's mom had called her husband. I waited until he arrived. As I was leaving, one of the technicians said, "Mr. Levin, thank you for what you did." I answered, "Thank you, but I didn't save the dog. You did."

Dusty is still alive. He recently survived cancer. Six months after the ordeal, he was walking again with a slight limp, as if nothing had happened.

When I got home that night, I told the family that Fran's dog had been hit by a car, had his leg broken, and that I helped them get him to the vet. Lauren later learned the details from Fran. She was very proud of her dad. The truth is that I did what every other dog lover would have done. There was nothing special about it. But it reminded me how fragile life is, particularly a dog's life. That day Dusty survived a car accident, a life-threatening injury, and delicate surgery. Another day it might be Pepsi. The experience brought me even closer to Pepsi, if that was possible.

The next day I saw Garrett. I thanked him and asked him how Pepsi had behaved.

"Well, Mr. Levin, he nipped me once, but only because I tried to pick him up. It wasn't anything serious." I laughed. "I guess he doesn't like to be picked up by strangers," I replied.

Pepsi is the perfect family dog. He's fun-loving, affectionate, and more obedient than your average teenager. And speaking of teenagers, he behaves like one of the kids. He thinks he's one of the kids, and so do we.

When Lauren and Chase have friends over, Pepsi joins in. He's part of every birthday party. During Christmas and Hanukkah, Pepsi looks forward to opening gifts like the rest of us. And when Kendall and the kids are sitting on the floor in the family room playing a board game, Pepsi makes his presence known by walking all over the board—messing up the cards and game pieces. I can hear them yelling at him now, "No, Pepsi!"

Pepsi has a very expressive face. He's a happy dog and he shows it. His eyes are big and bright. His ears rarely droop. He's almost always wearing a big smile, and his long, furry tail is constantly wagging. Well, actually, when he's really happy, his tail moves in a circle much like a propeller.

Pepsi's happy when we walk him, feed him

breakfast and dinner, give him a treat, or just give him attention. He loves taking drives in the car. He sits quietly on the front passenger seat (sometimes on the backseat), looking through the window as the world passes by.

When any of us comes home, as soon as we walk through the door Pepsi greets us. He becomes wildly excited and turns into what we call "devil" mode, sprinting around the house at warp speed, dodging the walls and furniture and us. We're always amazed at how he avoids slamming into something. I figure he's got some kind of built-in radar.

Like many dogs, Pepsi is no fan of the post-man or any other person delivering something to the house. He barks at them, leaving evidence of his breath on the glass windows around the front door, but he would never harm them. Pepsi's all bark but no action.

When he was young, Kendall taught Pepsi to fetch sticks and balls and play catch. He loves it. I don't think there are too many dogs who can catch a tennis ball as well as Pepsi. But once he catches the ball, he's not so willing to give it back. It takes a lot of coaxing and cajoling, but he eventually coughs it up.

In some ways Pepsi is still a puppy, especially when it comes to food—*human* food. I don't care where in the house he is, if he smells something going on in the kitchen, Pepsi shows up in a split second. He's looking for a scrap of food that may have been dropped on the floor or a chance to lick the dirty plates as they're loaded in the dishwasher. And, yes, I must confess, I toss him something from my dinner plate when no one is looking.

One time, when my parents were visiting, we were eating breakfast in the kitchen. My mother was talking and holding a piece of toast in her hand, waving it over the side of the table. Like a great white shark, Pepsi leapt for the toast and grabbed it out of my mother's hand. It only took a split second—and it was a clean grab! He never so much as brushed the skin on my mother's hand. She thought it was the funniest thing she'd ever seen. I was stunned. Pepsi had never been so brazen.

Since then, Pepsi has devoured a couple of hot dogs, slices of pizza, and a whole chicken. Once I found him with his face buried in a honey-baked ham, which had been left on the edge of the counter. Pepsi's also been known to eat candy. The evidence is usually found in the kids' bedrooms, where the empty wrappers are found on the floor. But the dog has an iron stomach. He can eat anything and rarely gets sick.

I know some perfectionists may find all this very disturbing, but Pepsi isn't always hunting for human food. His appetite is usually satisfied by the time he's done rummaging through the kitchen trash can for leftovers. And this is no small feat. The trash can is built into the cabinets, and you have to open a drawer to get to it. Pepsi figured this out right away. He pulls the drawer open with his paw and pulls the trash bag out of the can with his mouth. We've put magnets and child guards on the drawer, but none of it works. If we're not home to stop him, no obstacle is too difficult for him to overcome.

I see this as Pepsi training us. So now we clean up better after we eat and take the trash out more frequently. I really don't mind it very much, except for the occasional, inevitable gastritis attacks that hit him in the middle of the night. Good Lord! And he has no shame about it.

Pepsi receives a great deal of love and attention. Kendall takes him on car rides and to local parks, where she lets him run and plays catch with him. Every few months, she also takes him to be bathed and groomed. He comes home looking like a new dog. And Pepsi follows Kendall around, staying right on her heels as she moves from room to room.

Lauren and Pepsi have a special relationship. Lauren spends a lot of time with him when she's home. She cuddles with him on the sofa, talks to him in a sweet voice, and is always taking photographs of him. And Chase adores his "little brother," too. Pepsi often rolls on his side or back when he sees Chase approaching as he knows Chase will sit next to him and rub his chest and belly.

I hear people speak of the human-dog relationship as that of owner and pet. Of course we are the legal owners of Pepsi and he is technically our pet. But as any dog lover will attest, this doesn't accurately describe the relationship. Pepsi is an indispensable part of our family and our lives. His life is intertwined with ours.

When I take a ride down memory lane, Pepsi is there.

When I think about the future, Pepsi is part of it.

Goldfish, turtles, and hamsters are pets.

Dogs are family.

TWO

With Pepsi at My Side

February 2000

One winter day, during a lunch break, I was having Chinese food at a local restaurant with my dear friend, Eric Christensen. Eric and I grew up together in Elkins Park, Pennsylvania, just outside of Philadelphia. We're like brothers. I hired him as vice president for Landmark Legal Foundation, the public interest legal foundation where I am president.

In the middle of lunch I felt a sudden, sharp, intense pain in the center of my chest that literally jolted me. Eric said, "What's wrong?" "Hmmm, I'm not sure," I said.

A few seconds later it hit me again. "Eric, I'm having some kind of strange chest pains." Eric insisted we go to the emergency room. "Let's wait," I said. "If it happens again, we'll go." Almost before I could finish my sentence, I felt it again.

We quickly paid the bill and left for the closest hospital emergency room, which was Reston Hospital, only a few miles away. They ran me through a slew of tests. I hadn't had a heart attack. My vitals were fine. And I hadn't experienced any more chest pains. But the cardiologist who happened to be on duty at the hospital, Pradeep Nayak, insisted that I stay overnight. He also wanted to run some additional tests in the morning.

Little did I know that this was the beginning of an awful year in which I would be treated by a dozen cardiologists, take several ambulance rides to area emergency rooms, and undergo major life-saving surgery.

The next morning I was put through a treadmill test. A cardiologist hooked me up to a heart monitor to watch my heart's performance and rate when she increased both the speed and incline of the treadmill. After thirty seconds of walking, and before they increased either the speed or incline, my chest became extremely heavy and I was getting dizzy. "Let's stop. I can't do any more," I huffed. "That's the best you can do?" asked the doctor. "That's it," I replied. She said, "Well, this isn't good."

I'd been short of breath during the last few months, but hadn't given it much thought. I was out of shape, being twenty to thirty pounds overweight, and assumed that was the cause of the problem. But as I thought about it more, I remembered having great difficulty shoveling the snow off our driveway a few weeks earlier. It's a very short driveway and I had to stop several times to catch my breath. I also recalled struggling to keep up with Pepsi when we'd walk up steep roads. But it never occurred to me that I might have a heart problem.

Back to my hospital room I went. Dr. Nayak came by and said, "Look, we can do more tests. But I believe one or more of your arteries is blocked to some degree. I recommend we CAT you and get to the bottom of it." "What's a CAT?" I asked. "It's the gold standard for determining what's going on with your heart." He explained that they make an incision in your inner thigh and run a thin tube up your artery. They shoot dye through the tube to see if there are any blockages in the arteries leading to your heart. If there are, they use a balloon to open the artery, and sometimes implant a stent—a little wire tube—to keep it open.

It's not like I had a choice. We needed to know what was going on and fix it.

The procedure was not painful. They found two arteries that were partially blocked and implanted two stents. That should have done the trick. But ten weeks later, the chest pain returned, so back to the table I went. They found I had a problem with restenosis—in plain English, my arteries had already renarrowed around the stents. I was told that this occurs in about 15 to 20 percent of patients. Just my luck. I was one of them.

They inserted the tube up the artery in my thigh as before, but this time they used a tiny rotoblade at the end of the tube to drill through the blockages in the stents. About ten weeks later, the pain was back. I couldn't believe it. The stents were blocked again, and again the rotoblade was used to open them. I had a particularly aggressive form of restenosis. I knew this couldn't go on forever, and it didn't.

In June 2000, as I sat at my desk in my office, my chest suddenly felt like someone had dropped a ton of bricks on it. My breathing was labored. I knew I was in trouble. None of my colleagues were around as they'd gone to lunch. I had to get to the hospital and fast.

I worked my way down the stairs from my office to the parking lot. I managed to get into my car. At this point, the pain was excruciating. The hospital was just around the corner, but I was struggling to keep one hand on the steering wheel and stay on the road. My eyesight was getting blurry. I don't know why I didn't call 911. For some reason my instincts told me to drive myself.

When I got to the hospital, I couldn't find a parking space. I was driving through the lot, in obvious pain, and finally came across an empty space. As I pulled in, a man was watching me from his car. I got out of the car and said to him, "I think I'm having a heart attack." He said, "Get in!" He drove me to the emergency room entrance. Two paramedics happened to be there as they apparently had just finished dropping off someone else. They immediately took hold of me, put me on the gurney, and rushed me into the hospital. (To this day, I wish I knew the name of the pedestrian and paramedics who helped me. I don't even remember what they looked like.)

Wouldn't you know it? After they hooked me up to all the lines and monitors, the pain went away. I was lying in the bed joking with the nurses and doctor. But after a few hours of blood tests the report came back. I had had a mild heart attack. Some chest pain did return that day, but it wasn't as intense. Still, the doctors and I knew what had to be done. We had done everything possible to avoid bypass surgery, but the situation now compelled it.

I was moved by ambulance to Inova Fairfax Hospital, a top hospital in northern Virginia, where the surgery was scheduled for the next day. I spent the night in the intensive care ward just in case my condition warranted emergency surgery. I shared the room with a Baptist preacher. He slept most of the night. I couldn't. I was the first scheduled surgery in the morning. When morning came we introduced ourselves. He was going home. As it happened, they decided he didn't need an operation. As we talked, he learned that I was Jewish. He was from rural Virginia. He was a very pleasant and kind gentleman. I asked him if he'd say a little prayer for my family. I didn't fear death, but I worried about my family. He held my hand and prayed, "In His name, our Lord, Jesus Christ." I was more than thankful. At that point, I wanted to rally all the help I could get.

If you want to know what bypass surgery is like, just ask anyone who has had it. For several weeks after the surgery, you're in awful pain. Your chest has been cracked open and then put back together with stainless steel or titanium wires. I rejected most painkillers because they made me nauseous, and I would do anything to avoid the pain of leaning over a toilet and throwing up. I also had to sleep sitting up in bed or in a chair while clutching a pillow.

I had complications after my surgery. One of the grafts, or bypasses, failed. There was concern I'd have to go under the knife again. I would do anything to avoid that, and did.

I went through four or five more catheterizations and angioplasties over the next few months, including more ambulance rides to local emergency rooms. Kendall and I also went to the Cleveland Clinic, one of the best cardiac hospitals in the country, where they spent many hours working me over. But it was the guidance and expertise of my current cardiologist, Anne Safko, and a world-renowned cardiologist, Kenneth Kent, that got me through it all without further heart surgery.

"So what does this have to do with dogs?" you ask. Everything. Major medical problems take a grave toll on a family. My wife and kids went through a lot. Kendall was with me every step of the way. Lauren, who was twelve, and Chase, who was nine, would visit me in the emergency and hospital rooms. They had to deal with the stress of my heart surgery and help care for me when I came home. And they, like me, wondered what the future held for the family. They still worry about their dad.

During that miserable year, my Pepsi, only two years old then, was right there by my side, watching over me when I was home. He brought pleasure not only to me, but to all of us. And that's what dogs do. Life threw me a wicked pitch. I was literally fighting for my life. I felt like hell. And while I fought hard to recover, there were days when I thought I wouldn't make it. There were other days when I felt sorry for myself and sorry for the plight of my family. But as if to say, "Hey Dad, cheer up, the worst is behind you," there was Pepsi—snuggling up to me, licking my hand, wagging his tail, and always smiling. He would visit me as I lay in bed or sat in a chair, stuck on the second floor of our home. And if I was asleep or didn't notice him, Pepsi would make his presence known. He was such a welcome sight. He was ready to play. He was ready for a walk. He made me laugh even when laughing caused me considerable pain from the movement of my recently closed chest. Pepsi wanted his dad back.

During all the time I was gone from the house that year, Pepsi was also there for Kendall, Lauren, and Chase, reminding them in his way to be positive and live each day one at a time. After all, that's what dogs do, and he was a wonderful example to all of us.

Believe me when I tell you that he was a great motivating factor in my recovery. There is no question that Pepsi helped me get through the greatest challenge of my life. He was determined to get me back on my feet. Four weeks later, and ahead of schedule, that's what we did. I was still weak. I had lost a lot of muscle tone and weight (about forty pounds). But there we were, Pepsi and me, proudly—albeit slowly—walking down the street. At first we didn't get very far, but each day we made progress. The neighbors would wave and tell me how good I looked. They were just being nice—I looked terrible. I could tell they were shocked at how thin and pale I was. Still, life was finally getting back to normal.

As I became stronger, I got back into my routine, which, for me, included spending late nights in the basement on my computer. I do a lot of work and Internet browsing after everyone else goes upstairs to bed—everyone except Pepsi, that is. He has always kept me company, lying near my feet under the desk. After playing with a bone or ball for a while, he dozes off. Pepsi can be a loud sleeper. Sometimes he snores, like his old man. He dreams, too.

There are times when Pepsi spots a spider or some other bug out of the corner of his eye. We are in a basement, after all. That's when Pepsi's entertainment begins. Pepsi stretches out into a sphinxlike position, with his backside up in the air and his front legs stretched forward. He then corners the spider and playfully paws at it. He has no intention of harming it. He's just curious and trying to move his new friend from side to side or catch it.

Inevitably, however, the spider is doomed. And Pepsi always looks disappointed about what he's done.

THREE

Rescuing Sprite

October 2004

If I'm not too busy on a Saturday or Sunday morning, I like jumping in the car and exploring the Virginia countryside. I find it relaxing.

I can do a lot of thinking, and it's fun to drive down unknown roads. There's so much history in Virginia, you never know what you'll find.

We used to live in Reston, Virginia, about twenty-five miles outside of Washington, D.C. In 1998, during one of these trips, I happened upon a new development being built along the Potomac River in Virginia. They had just broken ground, so there were no buildings, just a few trailers featuring various builders and their plans for the community. It was still heavily wooded, but you could see the beginnings of a golf course. There were only a few new roads cutting through the development. I followed one to its end. Then I got out of the car, walked toward the Potomac River, and found the location where they planned to build some homes on a bluff above the river. The view was fantastic. I decided at that moment that one day we would live right there, where I was standing.

We'd have to wait several years until the development would be built out toward the river. Like most developments, the builders wanted to save the best locations for last. They make more money that way. Who can blame them? But I was persistent. I must have made fifty trips to the area over the next few years. And we scraped together every penny we could in anticipation of the day when we'd be able to buy a house on that lot. Finally, in 2002, the property I'd been eyeing all this time became available—and we bought it.

Whenever you move, it's difficult emotionally. Kendall and the kids were reluctant to leave their friends. We had a very nice and comfortable home in a beautiful neighborhood with so many great memories. It was the only home Chase had known, and Lauren had spent most of her life there, too.

I knew the process of building a home would be arduous and stressful, but I never realized how overwhelming it could be. Dealing with a builder, county inspectors, and missed deadlines is like holding a second job. It was enough to give a person with a healthy heart a heart attack. We invested lots of time and savings in the project, but I knew the move was right for the family.

The home is built into the side of a steep, heavily wooded hill, at the bottom of which is a significant creek. Behind the house there's an unobstructed view of the Potomac River from nearly every room. There are also loads of children in the neighborhood and the schools are excellent.

There were several delays before our home was completed. We were told it would be built in eight or nine months. Fourteen months after it was started, we moved in— November 2003. Lauren had the toughest time adjusting to the move. It wasn't that easy on Kendall and Chase, either. But something would soon happen that would change all of that—something beautiful that would change our lives forever.

Unbeknownst to me, Kendall and Chase decided that Pepsi needed a furry friend. In the summer of 2004, they began searching for another dog. They'd been to the local shelter at the Loudoun County (Virginia) Humane Society at least a dozen times. Chase also searched the Internet looking for just the right dog to add to the family.

When they told me what they were up to, I assumed they were going through a stage or something. I didn't take it seriously and dismissed it. When it became clear they weren't kidding, I was concerned. I worried that Pepsi's happy life would be turned upside down by bringing another dog into the home, especially an adopted dog with an unknown and uncertain past, and whose personality was already developed. What if the dog turned out to be too aggressive? What if Pepsi became depressed or jealous? I had images in my head of a potentially disastrous situation in which we might have to return the second dog to the shelter shortly after bringing him into our home. I couldn't stand the thought. Why invite problems?

Although Pepsi got along extraordinarily well with dogs when he'd play with them *outside* the house, I remembered that the one time a dog was brought inside our house— when my brother Rob and his dog visited us from Florida—Pepsi got nervous and standoffish. He even had an accident in the house for the first time since he was a young puppy. Lauren shared my concerns.

Ironically, Kendall, who had serious reservations about bringing any dog into our home some years earlier, was now pressing for a second dog. And I, who had insisted that a dog would add so much joy to the family, was reticent.

I eventually, and reluctantly, visited the local shelter with Chase. I had never been to a shelter before. It was upsetting to see all the dogs and cats in small cages waiting for some family to adopt them. I wondered what these poor animals must be thinking. They were in a strange place surrounded by people and animals they didn't know. They must have been scared to death, longing to be home with their families. Most of them were separated from families that they thought had adored them. In any event, they were the only families they'd known from the time they were puppies or kittens. And what of those families who'd lost their dogs, wondering what had happened to their precious friend? I can only imagine the pain they must have been suffering. If only they could talk and tell us where they're from, I thought.

Don't get me wrong. The people who care for these lost souls are doing the Lord's work. They really are. They try to help and protect the animals in hope that each of them will eventually find a good home, if not their original home. Many of the dogs and cats have been rescued off the streets, where their fate could have been horrific. And the folks who work at these shelters, and watch the animals come and go on a daily basis, are among the finest, most compassionate people in our society. Imagine what they must feel as they deal with the endless cycle of lost pets. I could never do it.

The sad truth is that the vast majority of these beloved animals will never be reunited with their original families, and some will never be adopted. I suspect that many are destroyed, but I didn't want to know and didn't ask. I couldn't get these thoughts out of my head, so after a short while, I motioned to Chase that I wanted to leave.

Chase found him on the Montgomery County (Maryland) Humane Society (MCHS) web-site. According to their records, he was brought to the shelter on September 19, 2004. He had been found roaming the streets of Silver Spring, Maryland. His photo had been posted along with many other lost dogs. He was said to be three to six years of age, a white-and-tan-colored spaniel mix, and very friendly. Kendall called me over to the computer screen to look at him. She said they'd found the most beautiful dog she'd ever seen.

I took a quick glance, so quick I didn't get a good look at him. I reiterated that I was not keen about getting another dog. Frankly, I was torn. Even though my experience at the local shelter had opened my heart to the plight of these dogs, I told Kendall I still feared what might happen to Pepsi. As I look back, I also think I wanted to protect myself from getting emotionally attached to another dog. What if we adopted him but it didn't work out? What then?

The dog was in the humane society's foster parent program. Kendall contacted the foster parents—Suzanne and Thomas Gallup. They told her that she was the second person to inquire about the dog. That was all Kendall needed to hear. She kicked into high gear. Within days, Kendall and Chase drove to Maryland to visit the Gallups and the dog. They fell in love with him. Kendall already gave him a name—Sprite. She had wanted a Sprite to go with her Pepsi, and Sprite was the perfect color.

The Gallups liked Kendall. They told her that she was their likely first choice to adopt him, if all else went well.

The Gallups were required to meet the rest of our family and watch our interaction with the dog. I was still reluctant, but Kendall was insistent. So, in the next day or two, Kendall, Chase, and I—and, oh yes, Pepsi—

piled into the car and started a journey I would never have anticipated.

Even the drive to see the dog was memorable. We took the White's Ferry across the Potomac River from Virginia to Maryland. I knew the ferry existed, but I'd never used it. It didn't seem like the most secure way to cross the river. It is the oldest and only ferry left to cross from Virginia to Maryland.

I drove the car onto the ferry, which was really a steel barge. They charged six dollars for a round trip. A single cable guided the barge from one side of the river to the other. It was powered by some kind of clunky, loud engine. It was all very quaint, and I wondered if we'd actually make it to the Maryland side. Kendall had already taken this trip a few times, and would take it many more times in subsequent weeks. I remember there was a snack bar on the other end. If I'd been on my own I probably would have stopped there. But Kendall doesn't want me eating junk food.

We drove for what seemed like a long time on a narrow winding two-lane road. The first leg of the trip took us through Poolesville, Maryland. We drove through mostly farmland with small, older homes dotting the road along the way. It was early October and the colors were beginning to change. I had no idea such a large rural area existed across the river not far from where we lived. After all, we hadn't been in our new neighborhood very long.

We eventually reached suburbia and a maze of roads and developments, which all looked alike to me. I seem to recall we made a wrong turn here and there. Once we arrived at the right street, Kendall pointed to the house. It was a nice neighborhood. The homes were about ten years old and well kept. The Gallups' home shared a cul-de-sac.

When we pulled into the driveway I was actually nervous, which was strange considering I thought I hadn't wanted another dog. But I'd come this far—the trip had taken about an hour—which suggested I was open to the idea after all.

I remained cautious about what I was getting into. As we reached the front door, with Pepsi tagging along, I told Kendall and Chase that there was no guarantee we were going to adopt the dog. They weren't paying much attention to me. They'd already gotten me this far and I guess they figured I had already relented.

The Gallups greeted us at the door. They, too, seemed a little nervous, but they couldn't have been kinder. It takes a special family to take in lost dogs and cats. They open their home and hearts to these helpless animals, they care for them, and then they have to let go of them to another family—who they also invite into their home. It can't be easy.

The Gallups walked us through their house and into the kitchen, which led to the backyard. I couldn't believe it. I was now *excited* about meeting the dog. They owned an older, friendly golden retriever.

As we went outside I immediately spotted Sprite! That wasn't his original name, of course. Nobody knew what that was. The Gallups were calling him Cody. But he was already "Sprite" to us.

My God, was he gorgeous! He had big brown eyes. His chest, much of his legs, and his face were white. His back, hips, and tail were tan. And, yes, he had that little white bobbed tail—it couldn't have been more than four inches long. His appearance reminded me of a fawn, especially the shape of his head and snout. But I couldn't stop admiring his magnificent eyes. I knew why Kendall and Chase wanted him.

Sprite was hanging out in the backyard, mostly oblivious to everyone around him. He'd been through a lot. No one knew how long he'd been roaming the streets before he was found. He'd spent time at the shelter. He'd been with the Gallups for two or three weeks, and now we were there. I walked over and petted him. His fur was as soft as anything I'd ever touched. He was extremely well behaved and gentle. He wasn't hyper. He wasn't aggressive. And there was a warm calmness about him.

Sprite seemed mature beyond his estimated age. I would later tell Kendall that I doubted he was only three to six years old. He didn't look or act old by any means, but he didn't seem as young as Pepsi, who was six. It didn't matter. He was already part of our family.

We introduced Pepsi to Sprite. Pepsi's tail must have been wagging a hundred miles an hour. Pepsi was frolicking around the yard, greeting the other dogs and the people.

I followed Sprite as he walked around the yard. The perimeter of the yard was fairly lush with plantings and, as I recall, some woods, which Sprite was exploring. Pepsi would come over to me once in a while just for reassurance.

When we all returned to the kitchen, Sprite plopped down in a corner of the room. Suzanne told us that Sprite was a very cuddly dog. They had put him on their bed and slept with him a few nights. She told us that Sprite was her first foster dog. She really didn't want to part with him, and that if she hadn't been committed to being a foster parent she would have adopted Sprite herself. I could tell they were torn by the experience. It was easy to fall in love with Sprite. As we would soon learn, everyone who met him adored him.

As we were getting ready to leave, Pepsi accidentally stepped on Sprite's paw. To my astonishment, Sprite growled at him. Sprite didn't show his teeth. He wasn't aggressive in any way. It was just a short, muted growl, but I took note of it. And I was the only one to hear it.

When we got in the car to leave, I told Kendall and Chase that I was now an enthusiastic supporter of adopting Sprite. I did mention that growling incident. They didn't seem to think much of it and I dismissed it, too. It would be the first and last time I ever heard Sprite growl at Pepsi.

Only later would I learn why Sprite reacted as he did that day: he was suffering from severe arthritis, for which he hadn't been diagnosed and wasn't being treated.

Before we could take Sprite home for good, Lauren had to visit with the Gallups and Sprite, as well. She wasn't all that thrilled about it. She was still protective of Pepsi. Kendall took Lauren and her boyfriend, Dan Schneider, back to Maryland. Upon meeting Sprite, Lauren's fears also melted away. She and Dan saw what the rest of us had seen—a gentle, precious dog any dog lover would want in his family.

The Gallups formally recommended Sprite for adoption by our family. Kendall met them at the humane society, where Sprite was handed over to her. This had to be her fifth trip to Maryland in a week's time. But we weren't done yet. The MCHS would be sending a representative to our home in the next few days to see how the dogs and humans were getting along. I was very impressed with the care they took in placing the dogs with loving families.

In the meantime, I was thrilled at how well

Pepsi and Sprite were getting along. It was as if Sprite had always been part of our family. He was a little shy, but that would soon change. And Pepsi was his usual happy self, although during the first few days it seemed like he was wondering when Sprite would be leaving. It was our job to make both dogs comfortable with the situation.

We fed them together and walked them together. We played with them and talked to them. There was no tension between them. Of course, Sprite was in a new and strange place, and Pepsi was no longer the sole focus of our affections. But it was remarkable how neither dog sought to control the other. They just went with the flow. They were not only compatible but were bonding. It was obvious in those early days that Pepsi's happy-go-lucky personality and Sprite's easygoing personality were a perfect fit. And they'd become even closer over time.

On October 14, about a week after we brought Sprite home, we were visited by Ms. Robinson of the humane society. This was the final hurdle. I remember Kendall busily running from room to room, straightening things up. I told her to relax, there was no way we wouldn't pass their test. Ms. Robinson was pleased with what she saw. She spent time with Kendall as I saw no reason to hang around. She asked some questions, took a look around, presented Kendall with some final papers to sign, and then departed.

We were ecstatic—Sprite was now officially a Levin!

FOUR

A Frightening Halloween

October 2004

It was Halloween night. All seemed well. Kendall was handing out candy to the trick-or-treaters with one hand and talking to her sister, Shannon, on the cell phone with the other hand. I was working in my home office in the basement, putting the final touches on edits of my first book, *Men in Black*, about the Supreme Court.

Sprite had been with us less than three weeks, yet, in that short amount of time, his assimilation into our family could not have been easier. He was such a sweet dog. He was well behaved, tolerant, and a perfect buddy for Pepsi. Sprite did seem a bit disoriented at times, but nothing major. We attributed it to his new surroundings and a difficult month of bouncing from place to place.

But that Halloween would badly jolt us. As I was writing, I heard Kendall let out a scream. I ran up the stairs to the front door, where Kendall had been greeting the children. I saw her drop the phone on the floor and run to Sprite. Sprite had collapsed on the floor. He had dropped like a brick.

Something was terribly wrong with Sprite. His legs were unstable. His eyes were darting and glazed. And he was shaking. We thought he might be having a seizure.

I remembered there was an animal emergency hospital a few miles away. I had passed it repeatedly on my drive home. I quickly threw my coat on, picked Sprite up off the floor, and carried him to the garage. I placed him on the front passenger seat of my car and sped off to the hospital.

Along the way, all kinds of scary thoughts crossed my mind: Did he have a stroke? Maybe he had some kind of blood disorder. Perhaps he's just dizzy from adjusting to a new environment. I was very worried.

I got to the hospital within five minutes, although the drive seemed to last an hour. I carried Sprite from the car into the waiting room. He only weighed thirty pounds or so. Whatever the problem, Sprite seemed to have stabilized.

The technician at the front desk appeared to be in her twenties, but she was obviously quite experienced at her job. I told her what had happened. She began asking questions about Sprite's background. I explained that we'd had Sprite for less than three weeks and knew nothing of his past and little about his medical condition. She was very kind and pleasant, took down the information, and asked us to take a seat until a vet became available.

I moved the welcome mat from in front of the hospital's door to next to my feet where I was sitting. I placed Sprite there. Sprite was completely cooperative. He'd get up a few times to curiously sniff the scents left by all the other animals who'd been there before him, he never barked, and he never winced in pain.

The hospital wasn't crowded, but Sprite and I sat there long enough to see some patients come and go, and long enough for Sprite to leave a small puddle on the floor. I apologized to the technician, but she said it was no big deal. She pulled a mop out of the closet and cleaned it up, refusing to let me do it. She'd obviously done it many times before.

Sprite was now resting, patiently waiting his turn. He wasn't sleeping. He was observing the place. But he looked much better. I couldn't stop staring at him. There we were—in the emergency room—on Halloween. I couldn't stop thinking about the life he had lived that I'd never know about. I couldn't stop admiring his beauty and grace.

A lady walked into the hospital with her cat in her arms. She was very upset. The cat didn't show any outward appearances of injuries or illness. She sat in the lobby, holding the cat to her chest. She was hugging and stroking it. Sprite was curious, but didn't bother them. I had wanted to comfort the lady, but I didn't know what to say. And I didn't want to upset her beyond the grief she was already experiencing.

The lady and her cat were soon led to one of the examination rooms by the technician. Maybe fifteen minutes passed. The lady quickly walked out of the back room and headed straight for the front door. She was crying quietly and wiping her eyes as she left the building. I felt horrible for her. I whispered to the technician, "She had to put the cat to sleep, didn't she?" She gave me a sad look and said they did. It was all I could do to keep myself from tearing. I asked her, "How can you deal with this part of your job day after day?" She said, "It's the worst part of it. It's very difficult."

I was reminded again how little time we have with our beloved dogs on this earth. And although my bond with Sprite already ran very deep, my heart was forever seared with my love for him on that night. All dogs rely on their human parents to care for them—to make sure they are well fed, properly treated, and enjoy their short lives. In return, we get pure love, loyalty, and happiness. Sprite was

already part of the family. We were even calling him "Spritey" as often as Sprite. And I felt
as if I had known him all my life. I also knew
that I couldn't bear the thought of being without him.

It was finally our turn. I followed the technician into one of the examination rooms. A
veterinarian came over to Sprite and me and
asked if she could conduct some tests on
him without my being present. She wanted
to check his eyes and balance, among other
things, without his being distracted by me.
So I waited in the lobby.

I called Kendall and told her that Sprite
seemed to be okay, he wasn't collapsing,
and that he was with the vet.

The conditions that caused me to rush
Sprite to the hospital didn't reappear during
the vet's examination. She noticed some eye
movement, but only with sudden movement
and nothing remarkable. His heart rate and
pulse were good. The other tests she conducted didn't reveal any problems. The vet
told me she had taken Sprite outside and
walked him behind the building and he did
fine.

The vet wasn't sure what Sprite's problem
had been. She speculated that it could sim-

ply have been a dizzy spell or vertigo, maybe a middle ear infection, perhaps he had experienced some kind of trauma in the past, or maybe there was a neurological issue, such as an infection, inflammation, or a tumor. Frankly, I didn't know what to think. She prescribed various medicines for him, but we decided to observe him for the next few weeks before undertaking any major course of action.

The vet also told me that Sprite was much older than three to six years. She estimated he was over ten years old. I can't say I was surprised. I knew instinctively that he was older than Pepsi.

As we drove home from the hospital, the streets were dark. Halloween was over. The kids were off the streets. I patted Sprite's head and back as he sat quietly in the front passenger seat. I was both relieved and worried about Sprite. The vet's prognosis wasn't all that helpful, but it wasn't dire, either. But from that night forward, I always worried about Sprite. I wasn't obsessed about his health, but I knew that given his age, there would be many more visits to the vet and we'd have far less time to be with him than we'd previously thought.

* * *

Sprite had a second episode within two weeks of our hospital visit. After that, it never occurred again. Still, his two back legs seemed a bit wobbly.

Kendall and I decided Sprite needed a complete checkup. He was already scheduled to have a large cyst removed from his leg. Kendall trusted Dr. Norman Walters, a veterinarian at the Poolesville Veterinary Clinic in Maryland. She first met him when she picked up Sprite to bring him home from the humane society as we were required to get Sprite a basic exam within five days. As it happened, Kendall had picked the first veterinary office—Dr. Walters's office—she came across when driving Sprite home.

I never met Dr. Walters. Kendall told me he was great with Sprite. She liked him and his staff and their kindness toward Sprite. So she and Sprite took one last trip over that ferry and through the Maryland countryside to see Dr. Walters.

Dr. Walters conducted a thorough examination of Sprite. He removed the cyst, conducted blood tests, cleaned his teeth, looked at his ears, took X-rays of his chest, back, pelvic area, and legs, and conducted cardiac tests. In the end, the X-rays revealed that Sprite had arthritis in his back and hip, for which he would take medicine the rest of his life, and an ear infection. Dr. Walters also confirmed to Kendall that Sprite was an older dog. But the good news was that it appeared Sprite did not have any life-threatening problems.

When Kendall brought Sprite home that evening, he was wearing an Elizabethan collar, a fancy name for a blow-up plastic collar placed around his neck. It prevented him from chewing on the stitches in his leg, where the cyst had been removed. He was a good sport about it, as he was about most everything. It annoyed him, as it would anybody, but for the most part he tolerated it.

I can't imagine what must have been going through Sprite's mind and the various emotions he must have felt. He had to be confused and upset.

Over a two-month period he'd gone from living for years with his original family to suddenly wandering the streets. He'd been found and then processed through the humane society, where he had been handed from human to human. He had seen several veterinarians and went through a number of examinations and procedures. He had been poked with needles and thermometers.

It broke my heart then, as it does now, to think how he must have wondered about the whereabouts of his original family.

My family and I were committed to doing everything we could to bring joy and comfort to Sprite's life. And, of course, Pepsi would play a big role in it.

But the truth is, Sprite did more for us than we ever could have done for him.

FIVE

Inseparable from the Start

December 2004

With his Elizabethan collar now gone and his arthritis medicine seeming to lessen his

pain, Spritey was more mobile—which he would soon demonstrate.

It was early December and it had snowed very heavily. Lauren had a few friends at the house. One of them left the front door open. Sprite decided to make a run for it and he bolted out the door. Lauren's boyfriend, Dan, who earlier had removed his wet shoes and socks, chased after Sprite in his bare feet. Sprite didn't know Dan well, so he was probably worried that some strange kid was running behind him, hollering and trying to catch him. Eventually Sprite was cornered next to a house a few blocks down the road. He was ready to call it quits. Dan sat with him and petted him to let him know he didn't want to harm him. With his bare feet burning from the snow and freezing cold, Dan walked Sprite back to the house.

I showed up near the end of the commotion and was scared to death. I thought, Boy, this could have been a tragedy! I warned everyone that they couldn't leave the door open because this is how Sprite may have gotten lost by his original family. Obviously, he wasn't one of those dogs who knew how to find his way home. In our case, he'd only been living with us for two months and the neighborhood was still largely unknown to him, so he could easily have been confused. Anyway, I felt we'd dodged a bullet.

Sprite would never bolt out the door like that again, although he'd have his chances. Even when Kendall would sometimes take Pepsi and Sprite into our yard without a leash while she was gardening or for a quick bathroom trip, Sprite wouldn't try to run away.

A few weeks passed. It was our first Hanukkah and Christmas with Sprite. Kendall cross-stitched a stocking for Sprite, as she had for all of us over the years. She hung it on the fireplace mantel right next to Pepsi's. We filled the dogs' stockings with treats and bones and made a fuss over them. Chase put a Santa hat on Pepsi, his yearly tradition. It never stays there very long before Pepsi shakes it off. It lasted an even shorter time on Sprite's head. Before it was over, Sprite was covered in wrapping paper and the kids put a bow on Pepsi. Lauren was busy snapping pictures which, thank goodness, she loves to do, for without her photos many of the family's most important memories would not be recorded.

It was our best holiday ever. Not because of the presents or food, but because somehow—whether God's will or fate—we had been blessed with our precious Sprite. Some might say we rescued him from an uncertain future. Maybe so, but I believe he was a magnificent gift to us. We were so fortunate and we knew it.

Most people dread walking their dogs. Not me. I have never viewed it as a chore. It gave me lots of time with Pepsi and Sprite. I walked the dogs every morning and night. When I'd wake up, no matter how difficult the day was going to be, I'd take great pleasure in seeing Pepsi and Sprite. Sometimes they greeted me, other times I had to wake them.

It soon became obvious that Sprite was hard of hearing. Kendall felt he was almost totally deaf. She would use a high voice to get his attention, but I would clap my hands to catch his notice if he was in another room. Some mornings, when I was on the main level of the house and Sprite was still upstairs, I'd clap to get Sprite to come down the winding front steps. He'd stop at the top of the staircase, wait for me to show him a treat, and then come bouncing down the steps. Pepsi was already at the front door (he'd get a treat, too).

Once downstairs, Sprite would then put his head down, right up against the door, signaling he was ready to go.

Like all dogs, Pepsi and Sprite loved their walks. It doesn't take much to make a dog happy: just the little things, the basic things. It is an important life lesson dogs teach us, and my dogs taught me: Career and financial goals are important, material acquisitions are necessary, but taking stock in life's little pleasures is the most satisfying experience of all.

During our walks I would observe how Pepsi and Sprite interacted with each other, strange people and dogs, and nature's little surprises. We had our routines. On the weekdays my time was limited, so I usually walked the dogs in our backyard and partly down a hill along the golf cart path. There was plenty for Pepsi and Sprite to see and smell. They'd check out the perimeter of the woods near our house. I could tell if deer, squirrels, skunks, red foxes, or some other wild animals had been there late the night before. I would have some difficulty getting the dogs to focus on doing their business as they'd try to enter the woods.

I was always a bit nervous at night. Even

though I'd put on the outside lights and carry a flashlight, I was never sure what creature might be stirring in the woods. Sometimes I could hear a deer barking warnings to the herd (we have a lot of deer around here and, yes, they do bark).

One night I had taken Pepsi's leash off and he heard a barking deer and sprinted off into the direction of the noise. I was terrified. I yelled for him loud enough to wake up the entire neighborhood. I tried to follow him, with Sprite in tow on his leash. I knew that Pepsi just wanted to explore and would only try to sniff the deer, but I also knew that a large deer could kill Pepsi with one deadly kick from his hoof. I couldn't see Pepsi or the deer.

Pepsi must have thought better about what he was doing and returned to me. Another potential disaster averted. I never again let Pepsi loose at nights.

Why, you might ask, did I let Pepsi off his leash if he might run? Well, I didn't do it often and I had no idea he'd run off. He hadn't done it before. But Pepsi is very particular about where he leaves his messes. He has to find exactly the right spot. This can go on for some time. I always felt he needed a little more room to roam, but I learned my lesson.

Sprite, on the other hand, would do his business literally within moments of my taking him outside. Whoever his original owners were, he apparently had been well trained.

I especially liked walking the dogs on the weekends. I'd take them down a fairly steep hill on the golf cart path along the river, not too far from our house. We'd cross over a small wooden bridge and there was plenty of time and room for them to walk, trot, smell, wee, poop, and generally explore.

We'd come across other dogs and their owners. Although Sprite was no danger to them, he was at times wary of strange dogs. Sprite was just being cautious. I would hold Sprite's leash tightly until he had a few seconds to get used to the dog. Kendall and I believe it was possible that Sprite may have been hurt by a dog or been in a bad fight sometime during his life. There were other indications, including a few small nicks on his ears. We had no way of knowing, of course.

But Sprite never attacked or harmed anyone or anything—not at the shelter, the foster parents' home, or our home. Despite all he had obviously been through, I never met a friendlier dog.

Walking back to the house was much tougher as we had to climb the hill. Sprite and I were worn out by the time we reached our backyard. Pepsi was still full of energy. He'd turn on his "devil" mode, race around the yard, and then head for the door.

Nothing brought more joy to me than to watch when Sprite, on occasion, would copy Pepsi's running. Although he was riddled with arthritis, Sprite ran toward the house while sprinting in circles and weaving in and out. He didn't do it all the time because he physically couldn't. But when he did, I would know that Sprite was feeling better. I also knew he was happy.

Sprite had a beautiful way of running. His thighs were muscular but his hind legs were somewhat short. He could be extremely fast when he was feeling well—faster than Pepsi. I suppose I would characterize it as running with a hop. Kendall also encouraged Sprite to run around the family room with Pepsi by leading them in laps around the coffee table.

When Sprite wanted a treat or to go outside, he'd let me know by running up to me, getting my attention, and then running toward the pantry or door. It was his way of saying, "Follow me!"

Pepsi loves walks in the snow. He runs through the snow, eats snow, and pushes his snout into holes in the snow to inhale the fresh air. Sprite, on the other hand, was not a fan of the snow. In fact, I don't think he was a fan of the cold weather at all, no doubt because of how it affected his arthritis. I remember during our first winter with Sprite, I walked Pepsi and him out back and after a short while Sprite was lifting one of his paws in pain. I picked him up and carried him to the house. I noticed there were areas on the pads of his paws that were worn. After that, I limited his walks in the snow.

When the weather was nice, I would sit on the lawn in our backyard, above the Potomac River, with Pepsi on one side of me and Sprite on the other. We would relax, watch the golfers, and, most of all, enjoy the breeze. There always seems to be a breeze where we live. Maybe it's caused by the river. I haven't bothered to figure it out.

No one appreciated a nice breeze more than Sprite. He would lift his head, turn toward the breeze, and become mesmerized by it. When I walked him and a breeze started up, he would stop in his tracks and face toward it. I couldn't move him if I wanted to. Instead, I learned to slow down and enjoy it with him.

Breezes tell dogs a million stories we humans can never know. Their sense of smell is orders of magnitude more sensitive than ours. In Sprite's case, he actually seemed to be reflecting on what he was feeling and experiencing rather than merely reacting to it. This was his nature. When you talked to Sprite, he would look at you as if he were trying to understand what you were saying, not just listening for commands and praise. Pepsi has a similar way about him. Perhaps that's why they were so compatible.

I would often get down on the floor, hold either Pepsi or Sprite's head in my hands, and put my nose up against their nose. I would tell them how beautiful they are, how much I love them, and kiss them on the nose. They would stare into my eyes and seem to know exactly what I was saying and feeling. And I knew they loved me, too.

Dogs by nature are territorial. By all rights, Pepsi could have been aggressive had he seen Sprite as an intruder. It never happened. Pepsi welcomed Sprite into his life. Neither Pepsi nor Sprite tried to be the alpha dog. And neither was submissive, either.

They became very close very quickly. The relationship developed into a father-son or older brother-younger brother bond—Sprite being the older. As they got to know each other, Sprite would affectionately lick Pepsi, usually on the top of his head but also all over his fur. Sometimes Sprite would give Pepsi such a long bath that Pepsi would look at me as if saying, "Can you tell him to stop now?" But every now and then, Pepsi would reciprocate. This was all the more remarkable as they were mature dogs who hadn't been together that long.

Pepsi likes to eat grass on our walks, a habit Sprite picked up from him (although no dog can graze with Pepsi's gusto). Until he met Pepsi, I'm sure it never crossed Sprite's mind to supplement his diet this way. Now they could both throw up together.

As time went on, Sprite had more difficulty walking up that hill in the backyard, so I began walking the dogs around the front yard and down the street more often. We saw many more neighbors—of the human and dog variety—and we became somewhat of a fixture.

My friend Bill Berry, who is also a dog lover and has a pup named Rickey, would comment how he always saw me walking the dogs and how lucky they were to have me. It was always nice to hear that from Bill. But I knew I was the lucky one.

The neighborhood is full of young kids. When they'd see us they'd call out Pepsi's and Sprite's names and run over to pet them. The dogs loved the attention and were always very good with kids. The neighbors saw the dogs as inseparable, and inseparable they became.

While I spent a lot of time with Pepsi and Sprite, Kendall spent all day with them. Pepsi and Sprite followed her all over the house, from bedroom to laundry room, from living room to kitchen. She was their mom. She played with them, took them on drives, brushed them, and took them to be groomed. Kendall once picked them up at the pet groomers after they had been bathed and trimmed and the groomer told her that the dogs wanted to be in the same cage together. What a pair!

Pepsi has his own warm-up exercise when he wakes up or is ready to go out: He stretches his front legs and sticks his hind quarters up in the air. Sprite picked up on this and would do the same, when he was feeling well enough. And during Pepsi's raids on the trash can in the kitchen, Sprite became a willing accomplice. Pepsi would drag the trash bag into the family room, where they would proceed to devour every vaguely edible morsel of food. They also hunted the trash cans and tabletops in Lauren's and Chase's bedrooms for candy. We rarely caught them in the act, but they didn't cover their tracks very well, and they always looked guilty as hell. When we'd come into the room after one of these episodes, Kendall would simply look at Pepsi, and he'd walk into the bathroom to punish himself. I don't know what Sprite's prior experience was, but he must have delighted in the bounty he found in his new home.

Pepsi and Sprite had different eating habits. They had separate water and food bowls, but they were placed next to each other so they stood together as they ate. When we fed them their dog food, Pepsi wolfed his down so fast I doubt he could taste it. I'm not even sure he chewed before he swallowed. Sprite was a slow eater. He liked to savor. He would pick through his food, decide which morsels were the tastiest, and he'd eat those first. The morsels he liked least were placed on the floor next to his bowl, and he might or might not get to them. If he left them, Pepsi would vacuum them up. Pepsi might or might not drink some water after he ate. Sprite would always take a slow drink after his meals.

Their sleeping preferences were also different. Pepsi usually slept under the night table or behind the curtains near the bed. Sprite liked to nest on clothes, blankets, and soft doggie rugs. We placed them on his favorite spots throughout the house. Pepsi didn't move around much at night. Sprite would usually start out at the foot of our bed and wind up in one of three or four different places. One morning I found him resting on a pile of dirty clothes in the laundry room.

Many times Sprite slept on the second-floor landing outside our bedroom, which was at the top of the stairs. From that location, Sprite had a bird's-eye view out the picture windows at the front and back of the house. I remember many times when Sprite would bark in the middle of the night or early in the morning at the light reflecting off the river from the water tower on the Maryland side of the Potomac. Other times he'd bark at the trees silhouetted against streetlights out front.

When he'd do that, I'd hop out of bed and lie next to Sprite. I'd start rubbing his chest and he'd roll over onto his side. I'd whisper to him that all was well and he'd relax and soon start to fall back to sleep. When I'd head back to bed, he'd lift his head, glance at me, and then put it down again. He was reassured and so was I. He was nesting like a little fawn.

Sprite loved to be held, and we loved to hold him. We would put him in our laps and hold him close to us. Sometimes Kendall and I would put him on our bed. He reveled in close contact and had a unique appreciation for affection. Pepsi is also affectionate. And the more he was around Sprite, the more he was able to express it.

Pepsi and Sprite were always greeting people at the door. If they heard a car or delivery truck in the driveway, they would take up positions on either side of the front door, look out the windows, and bark at the approaching person as their tails wagged at the speed of sound. It was easy to tell their barks apart as Sprite's bark was deeper than Pepsi's.

When they both barked at the same time, it was like music to my ears. I knew this was the way it was supposed to be.

The dogs would make a fuss over almost anyone who came to the house, but they had their favorites. My father, Jack, who now lives in Florida with my mother, is unable to visit us often. But when he did, Pepsi and Sprite loved being around him. My dad gave them attention, was gentle with them, and spoke to them in a soft, friendly tone. Dogs can tell when they're around dog lovers, and my dad is a dog lover. The same can be said for my brother Doug, who visits us from Philadelphia a few times a year. Doug is tall and can look intimidating to a dog, but they quickly find he's soft-spoken and easygoing. Pepsi and Sprite were always excited to see him.

Pepsi and Sprite also adored my childhood friend Eric Christensen. Eric grew up without any siblings. When we were children, he'd often come to our house not only to play with my brothers and me, but to see our dogs Prince and Lady. I remember some thirty years ago when Eric showed up at our house one day with his own puppy. He picked her up from a shelter. She was a Jack

Russell mix. He named her Muffin. To this day, Eric talks to me about her. You never forget a beloved dog, I don't care how much time passes.

Eric always made Sprite and Pepsi feel special. He took time to play with them and praise them. He knew how and where they liked to be rubbed. Eric has a way with dogs that few others do. He understands they have individual personalities and feelings, and he pays attention to them. When Eric would come to the house, Pepsi and Sprite knew they were going to have some fun with a good friend. They were always thrilled to see him.

And our next-door neighbors—Maurico and Renata Mendonca, and their children, Luiza, Julia, and Daniel—are dear and rare friends. We've only known them since we moved to our new house over three years ago. They had known Sprite since we first brought him into our family. They're originally from Brazil and are very warm people. We feel like we've known them forever. The Mendoncas have their own dog, a dachshund named Maggie. Maggie would run over to play with Sprite and Pepsi when I'd take them outside.

Whenever we would go out of town to visit family or take a vacation, we would ask the Mendoncas to care for Pepsi and Sprite. They became close to the dogs, and we knew they'd be in good hands. They never turned us down. I didn't want to leave the dogs at a kennel or any other strange place. Pepsi wasn't used to it, and Sprite had been through enough way stations. I wanted them to remain in the house and be in their familiar surroundings when we weren't around.

Before we left on a trip, we always made sure the house was safe, the thermostat was properly set, and there were enough lights on so the dogs could find their way around. I even began to leave the toilet seat covers up as I noticed that Sprite would sneak a rare drink from the toilet bowl every now and then. I guess it was a habit he began with his original family. We also left a long "to-do" list that covered everything from which medicines to give the dogs to various emergency phone numbers. And I always carried the Mendonca's phone numbers in my wallet.

When we'd return home, Pepsi and Sprite would meet us with big smiles on their faces. Pepsi could barely contain his excitement, sprinting from family member to family member. Sprite would come up to us and press his head against our legs, an incredibly tender act. He'd do it frequently to family and friends. Later, Pepsi would emulate it.

From December of 2004 to December of 2005, Sprite's health was fairly good. There were no serious problems. I still wondered about his life before us. Sprite was such a well-behaved and loving dog. He had even been trained by his original family to give his paw on command.

But there was one reaction Sprite had that always bothered me. Whenever we would slowly reach to pet him on his snout or head, Sprite would shutter or flinch. Pepsi never reacted that way. And, of course, we never, ever hit Sprite or gave him any reason to be fearful. So I wondered whether he had been abused by others—whether his snout had been smacked when he barked or for some other reason. I prayed he was not mistreated before he came into our family, and I don't know that he was. But the mere thought was hard to take.

SIX

Dinner with Pepsi and Sprite

December 2005

I broadcast my radio program from my office in the basement of my house—"the concrete-and-steel bunker," as we call it. One of the benefits, of course, is that it allowed me to spend much more time with the dogs than if I had to travel each day to a studio in Washington, D.C.

I would get home from working at Landmark Legal Foundation around 4:00 P.M. to do my final show prep for the day. Each afternoon I'd pull into the garage, enter the house, and Pepsi and Sprite would greet me as if I'd been gone for weeks. I'd hug them and give them big kisses. And they knew what was coming next—I would go to our walk-in pantry to get them a treat.

Pepsi and Sprite would sit at the pantry door waiting for me to reappear. When I did, they'd focus on me like a laser, looking straight into my eyes with great anticipation. I'd throw Pepsi his treat, which he'd easily catch. And I'd put Sprite's treat on the floor, which he'd gobble up. I might also get in an extra walk with them if Kendall wasn't around to do it.

As I would head for the basement, the dogs would follow. Sprite had a particularly neat way of presenting himself as he came down the basement stairs. When he would reach the basement floor at the bottom of the steps, it was almost as if he would announce himself with a "ta-da!" Unlike the main level of the house, which has mostly wood floors, the basement has thick carpeting and Sprite didn't have to worry about slipping or falling. He would march around happily for a few brief seconds. In the meantime, Pepsi would already have scooped up the closest ball or bone.

I spend a great deal of time in my home office. It's where I do most of my radio-show preparation. And it's where I do most of my writing for articles and books.

There's nothing flashy about my office. It's like most others, except for the addition of a microphone, headphones, and a "Zephyr"—a box full of electronic devices and wires connected to a phone line. I don't pretend to know how all this works, but somehow the Zephyr enables me to broadcast to millions of people across the country. Before and during my show I constantly monitor the news, both on my computer and television, to make sure I am up to speed on any breaking stories.

Sprite and Pepsi would typically spend an hour or more sitting with me in my office as I planned each day's radio program. Pepsi would lie next to my desk and Sprite would plop himself down on the soft rug I'd put a few feet away from the desk. And they'd rest there until they heard someone come home.

About thirty minutes before my show started I would have to usher the dogs out of my office and shut my door to prevent any noise from distracting me or making it on the air. But it didn't always work.

The basement is lined with windows, so you can see the golfers and golf carts move along the path with the river behind them. Many times during my show, I could hear the dogs bark at the golfers. When they were especially loud, I knew some hacker was in my backyard retrieving his ball.

I always wondered whether the audience could hear the barking. Rich Sementa, my producer and engineer, swore they couldn't, but every now and then I'd accidentally leave the door open. Then I knew their barking could be heard from coast to coast. I would usually joke about it.

I had no idea at the time, but my radio audience was developing a relationship with my dogs.

When nobody was home but the dogs and me, Pepsi and Sprite would lie outside my office door during the entire two-hour broadcast, waiting patiently for me to finish.

When the show was over, I'd open the door, they'd jump up, and I'd make another fuss over them—thanking them for being there for me. We would then head upstairs to the kitchen, where they'd join me for dinner.

If Kendall was home, the dogs would usually follow her around the house during my broadcast. As the kitchen is located above my basement office and I broadcast during dinnertime, I could hear the pitter-patter of the dogs' paws on the wooden floor as Kendall was making dinner and the dogs were following her around the kitchen. Pepsi and Sprite had distinctive walks. Sprite took smaller steps than Pepsi, so I could tell which dog was walking at any given time.

Most nights the family had already eaten by the time my show was over. If Kendall was home, she and the dogs would usually be in the master bedroom, where she'd be reading, watching TV, working on a jigsaw puzzle, or folding laundry.

As difficult as it was for Sprite to hear, he knew when I was getting my silverware and plate of food from the warming drawer. He'd come bouncing down the back stairs, leading from the second floor to the main floor. Pepsi would show up, too, although he managed to get to the kitchen from a different route.

This was our routine almost every night. And it was *always* the highlight of my day. Sprite and Pepsi were my dinner partners. They kept me company. Sprite would put his head on one of my legs and stare at me as I ate. He was so excited about getting a scrap of human food that his body would shake. Sometimes he couldn't stand very long as his arthritic legs would begin to weaken, so he'd lie on the floor next to me. Pepsi, who'd be sitting next to my other leg, also waited for a taste of my dinner. If Sprite moved to my other leg, Pepsi would get out of the way and switch positions with him.

Just as Pepsi and Sprite had different eating habits, they had different table manners. I'd toss Pepsi a small bite of food and, of course, he'd catch it before it could hit the ground. If I had thrown food at Sprite, it would have just hit him in the head and fallen to the floor. Sprite not only had better table manners, but given his age and health he didn't have Pepsi's mobility, so I'd drop it on the floor near him.

While eating I would talk to my two dinner companions.

"Did you have a good day?"

"Did you behave?"

"Anything new going on?"

"You look so beautiful today!"

I'd tell them about my day or some event in our lives. They'd look at me inquisitively, or maybe like I was nuts. And after dinner, I would take them out for their last walk of the day.

Sprite and Pepsi also could tell when any of us were a little down or just needed some love and attention. For instance, during much of 2005 I had been suffering from plantar fasicitis in my right foot—that's pain in the band of tissue connecting the heel bone to the base of the toes. By early December it had become unbearable. It's not an uncommon problem and is usually responsive to remedial treatments—but not in my case. The problem persisted for months, by which time I was walking with a cane and limping badly. I decided I had no choice but to have surgery.

It was a relatively minor outpatient procedure. My doctor cut the band, put a few stitches in my foot, placed some gauze on it, wrapped it in an Ace bandage, and told me to stay off my foot for two weeks. I was prescribed a powerful painkiller and antinausea medicine, which I used only a couple of times. We have a guest bedroom in the basement and a full bath, so I moved down-stairs for the two-week duration.

I would use either crutches, crawl, or hop to get around. The guest bedroom is only about twenty feet from my office, so there was no problem broadcasting while I was recovering. Once I worked my way over to the desk, I was set. Everything I needed was there.

Kendall took good care of me. She and the kids would visit me, but I was stuck in the basement. I'd get bored. I wanted to take a drive, which I often do at night. It helps me relax after a thirteen-hour workday.

When I wanted to leave the basement, it took a lot of effort to drag myself up the stairs to the main floor. Once I fell headfirst down the stairs on my way back to the base-ment when I stupidly tried using my crutches on the steps. I received some deep gashes on my leg and elbow, and I didn't try it again.

But just when I'd start feeling sorry for myself, lying in bed watching TV or reading a book, my two favorite furry buddies would visit me. In fact, once they realized they could find me in the basement, and that I was sleeping there, they came to see me all the time. Some nights they would sleep next to my bed. I can't tell you how satisfying it was when, in the middle of the night, I'd look over my shoulder and see Sprite or Pepsi or both sleeping on the floor next to the bed.

There is nothing like the loyalty and love dogs have for their families. Nothing.

It had been over a year since Sprite had collapsed. Since then, there had been no major medical episodes. His arthritis had become extremely severe—from his neck to his back and into his hindquarters—and we worked with the vets to find the best combination of medicines to help him. Some of the medicines made him sick or dizzy, so we'd stop them. We always came back to Rimadyl, which gave him some relief, although we never knew how much.

There were those days when Sprite would tire easily and slow down. That's what older dogs do. But for the most part, he would join in the fun and activities around the house, or at least try to.

It was now late December of 2005, and events were about to take a turn for the worse.

SEVEN

There Is No Forever

Late December 2005

It was Sprite's second Hanukkah and Christmas with us. As in most families, this is a special time in our home. Kendall works very hard to decorate the house for the holidays. We typically have our menorah on the countertop not too far from the fireplace, where the stockings are hanging. Kendall also likes to bake, so there's always an abundance of food to nibble on.

I remember thinking on this particular holiday how fortunate I had been that year: My book had done very well. I was also a few weeks away from completing contract negotiations with the ABC Radio Networks to syndicate my radio show, and Landmark Legal Foundation had experienced its most successful year in its thirty-year history.

But these career accomplishments, while gratifying, weren't what made the year so special. It was the wholesomeness of our family, thanks to the addition of our Spritey, who had become such an integral part of our daily lives. He was Pepsi's pal, a cherished companion for Kendall, a happy and loyal friend for Lauren and Chase, and a shining light in my life. It seemed as if Sprite had always been there. I couldn't imagine our family without him. I looked at Pepsi and Sprite and marveled at how close they had become and how easily Sprite had adapted to our home.

Sprite's kindness, beauty, and affection won us all over. Despite the fact that he had lost his original family and had to deal with severe arthritis—emotionally and physically wrenching challenges most of us would have great difficulty overcoming—he was a joyful soul who was friendly to anyone who would take a moment to acknowledge him, talk to him, or pet him.

This was such a special holiday. As I took stock of our many blessings, I thought to myself that life doesn't get any better than this.

But a few days later, life was about to deliver a crushing blow that would shake my faith and my ability to cope as nothing else before.

I don't remember the exact date, but I was walking through the foyer, the sun was shining brightly into the house, and Sprite came up to me. I couldn't believe my eyes. I noticed immediately that the right side of his head, just above the eye, was badly indented. And his right eye appeared somewhat sunken into the eye socket. I literally had to catch my breath. I couldn't believe it. I held his head in my hands, took a closer look, and began to tear up. At that instant I knew we were in trouble.

Kendall and the kids would soon be returning home from Huntsville, Alabama, where they had participated in my sister-in-law Ashley's wedding. I called them to tell them something was terribly wrong with Sprite. As soon as Kendall came home and saw him, she said with a stunned look on her face, "Oh, no! What happened?" I told her it just happened, but I didn't know why or how. Sprite was also rubbing his right eye frequently with his paw, or rubbing it against the sofa or our legs. He didn't seem in pain, but it was clearly irritating him.

We got Sprite to the Old Mill Veterinary Hospital in Leesburg, Virginia. Dr. Jessica Plant, who had taken wonderful care of Sprite and Pepsi during most of their visits for the past year, had a special way of talking to our dogs that put them at ease. She was compassionate and they trusted her. But she wasn't in that day.

Dr. Judy Bardsley was the first to see Sprite. We didn't know her well, but her kindness and professionalism was immediately apparent. She realized the seriousness of Sprite's condition the moment she saw him. After she examined Sprite, Dr. Bardsley characterized his condition as "pronounced masseter muscle atrophy," a severe shrinkage of the muscles on the right side of his face. She scheduled X-rays and a muscle biopsy.

Dr. Chris Hussion was on duty during the day of the tests. He reviewed Dr. Bardsley's notes and decided to consult a neurological expert. The neurologist believed an MRI would be the logical next step. He felt it was highly likely that Sprite had a tumor not of the brain, but on the nerve that controlled the muscle on the right side of his face. Dr. Hussion also explained that if we did an MRI and found a tumor, we would have to be prepared to put Sprite through surgery and a series of treatments that might degrade his quality of life if not kill him. He was especially concerned about the use of anesthesia, which would have to be administered each time Sprite was treated. He also estimated Sprite's age to be thirteen or fourteen years old, maybe older, which was a complicating factor. Dr. Hussion said the neurologist suggested we could try giving Sprite prednisone, a form of steroid, which might provide some help.

Our family was in disbelief. This was a lot to digest. I had tried to put Sprite's mortality out of my mind since that Halloween over a year earlier when he first collapsed. There was no way to avoid it anymore. The prognosis wasn't good. We had to face the fact that Sprite was old and ill, and there weren't any good options. We wanted to do whatever was best for him, and most of all, we didn't want him to suffer.

Another thought crossed my mind: I remembered back when I was around twenty years old, and our beloved dog Prince became ill. I remembered that my parents did everything they could to save him. I never knew the details of what occurred, except that Prince received the best medical attention available at the time. But he suffered during his last days.

Not long ago, I asked my parents about Prince's death. My mother told me that when Prince turned around twelve he began losing most of his fur. His exposed skin was sore and his back had developed cuts. They took Prince to the School of Veterinary Medicine at the University of Pennsylvania, considered to be one of the best animal research and treatment institutions in the Philadelphia area. My dad said that the veterinarian they originally saw wasn't very compassionate but seemed competent. He prescribed some kind of experimental medicine. It wasn't long before Prince grew his fur back—thicker than before—but his health declined badly. My mother said they couldn't bear putting him down so they kept him alive much longer than they should have. In the end, she said, he suffered. And my parents regret it to this day. I could hear the anguish in my mother's voice as she spoke to me.

My dad and younger brother, Rob, who, like my older brother, Doug, is kind and good-hearted, eventually took Prince back to that hospital, this time to put him out of his pain. My father said that the vet on duty was a kind lady who took one look at Prince and said, "Good Lord, this dog is suffering terribly."

As advanced as medicine has become, Kendall and I worried about initiating a course of surgery and treatments that would damage Sprite further or cut his life short. I assumed Sprite had a tumor, as did Dr. Hussion. At this stage of his life, there was no way we were going to put Sprite through the trauma of major head surgery.

We had been assured by our vets that the muscular atrophy was not causing him pain. He didn't seem to have any pain at all. And other than rubbing his eye, which could not be completely relieved but eased somewhat with drops and ointments, Sprite would probably be able to hold on for a while.

We gave Sprite the prednisone, which only made him sick. After a few weeks, we had to drop it. At that point, there was really nothing else we could do but love him and make the most of our time with him. There was no indication Sprite faced imminent death, but we also knew there was no forever.

As 2006 began, we went about our lives, of which Sprite was a primary part.

Along with the routine, it would be a memorable year, with several important milestones, and Sprite would share in all of them.

After months of negotiations, ABC launched my radio syndication. While a lot of my attention would be needed to ensure that it would be successful, I am always protective of my time with my family.

Despite enormous pressure to hit the road and court new radio affiliates, I did my best to limit those trips as much as possible. It's easy for many to get caught up in the glitz of "celebrity"—such as it is, in my case—or the popularity of the moment. But a phrase delivered by George C. Scott in my favorite movie, *Patton*, is one I've remembered since I first heard it at the age of thirteen: "Glory is fleeting." And I think it was a radio icon, the late Jean Shepherd, who put it even more starkly: Five hundred years from now, none of us existed. The moral for me is that your family is the most important part of your life. It is your legacy and your immortality.

During all the hours I prepared for my radio program and broadcast my show, Sprite and Pepsi were with me or near me, just as before. And we continued to have dinner together and go for nightly walks. But now they were more important to me than ever.

We celebrated Lauren's eighteenth birthday in March and Chase's fifteenth birthday in May. Sprite and Pepsi celebrated, too. Pepsi was born on July 7, 1998. We didn't know Sprite's birthday, so we'd have a party for him on the day we adopted him in October.

It was also the year Lauren graduated from high school. Kendall invited family, friends, and neighbors to an afternoon buffet at the house in Lauren's honor. She laid out a nice spread on the dining room table. It was a sunny and pleasant June day, so we opened the doors to the deck, which overlooks the river. Pepsi and Sprite had a blast roaming in and out of the house, meeting all the people, and picking up bites of food here and there from the plates that were left behind or which were accidentally dropped. And, of course, I would toss them a small piece of food when no one was looking.

As in the past, deliverymen and servicemen would come and go during the year, and Sprite and Pepsi would bark at them from the window, greet them when they walked into the house, and keep them company throughout the visit. The dogs were always glad to meet somebody new and they were always curious about what they were doing.

In the spring and summer, Sprite and Pepsi would continue to keep Kendall company as she'd plant flowers and tend to her garden, never wandering too far from her. They'd bark at the golfers through the basement windows as they did before. All was as it was.

But there was no ignoring that Sprite was gradually slowing down. His body was showing signs of aging, and the tumor was beginning to take its toll. Sprite's walk became more rigid. He was sneezing more often and was having miniseizures at night. They weren't life-threatening, but they were noticeable.

Through it all, Sprite never stopped enjoying life. He would still get excited about the little things—when we returned home, fed him, and gave him treats. He would still look at us with those big, beautiful eyes, affectionately lean against our bodies, and cuddle with us. And along with Pepsi, he would still wait at my office door during my radio show to join me for dinner when I was done broadcasting.

Although the good days far outweighed the bad, I couldn't stop thinking about the limited time we had left with Spritey. I would try to put it out of my head, but I couldn't. I would look at him for long periods of time—whether he was sleeping or eating, or sitting with Kendall and the kids, or lying next to my feet—and think what a precious gift he was to the family. He had such grace and dignity, despite all he had been through. I learned so much from him: about myself, about life, and about class. I learned so much from Pepsi, too—he was showing Sprite affection and companionship throughout, as Sprite was showing him. It was as if they knew.

During the summer, I struggled with my

emotions, mostly in silence. I knew what was eventually in store for all of us, and I had no good way to prepare for it. In the meantime, our family did what families do: We continued with life's daily routine.

During our many visits to the vet, I had seen a booklet on display on the far corner of the countertop in the receptionist's area. It was about end-of-life decisions for dogs and cats. I wasn't comfortable looking at it. I felt to do so would be to accept Sprite's fate, and I wasn't ready for that.

Then during one visit, I picked up the booklet. I didn't read it. I took it home and put it in my desk drawer.

Lauren had been accepted to the University of Alabama in Tuscaloosa, Kendall's alma mater. At first she was excited about the prospect of going away to school, living in a dorm, and being on her own. She had visited the school with Kendall, and it was located fairly close to Kendall's family. Lauren had even convinced her childhood friend, Ambre Rypien, to apply there and be her roommate. But as August arrived, and the time to leave for Alabama neared, Lauren started to get cold feet. She even confided in me that she had second thoughts about being so far from home.

There wasn't much I could do at this point. There were no other options as Lauren had already turned down offers from other schools. So I told her to try a semester and if she still wasn't happy, she could transfer to a college closer to home.

We decided that Kendall would take Lauren to school for her first weekend before classes started, and I would go there the following weekend. That way, Lauren might have an easier time settling in.

It was the end of August, the weekend before Labor Day. There are no direct flights from Washington, D.C., to Tuscaloosa. You have to fly into Birmingham and then drive sixty miles from Birmingham to the University of Alabama. But I couldn't even find a direct flight to Birmingham, so I wound up flying from Washington to Charlotte, from Charlotte to Birmingham, and then renting a car to get to my daughter's dorm.

During the short holdover in Charlotte, I killed some time looking in the shops. I came across a jewelry store that had on display small, ceramic pendants in the shape of various breeds of dogs. They were each hand-painted. I went in the store and bought two pendants that most closely resembled Pepsi and Sprite. I knew Lauren would miss the dogs; she adored them. I had hoped the pendants might help keep her company. When I finally got to Lauren and showed her the pendants, she was thrilled.

I spent two and a half days with Lauren, helping her organize her room, wash her clothes in the community laundry room in the dorm's basement, and pick up odds and ends at the local Target. I enjoyed our meals together and had a wonderful time with her. I am very close to Lauren, as I am with Chase. We share a special bond, as do many fathers and daughters. And truth be told, I was just as upset about leaving her as she was of leaving home. We were both putting on a good face. Lauren wanted to come home, and I didn't want to do anything to make her more upset by offering her false hope. She had to stick out the semester.

The day I was leaving, we spent time together in the morning in her dorm room. The time went quickly. During the short elevator ride to the lobby, I put my arm around her shoulder. When we reached the lobby, we headed for the front door. We stopped and hugged each other. We held on more tightly and longer than usual. Lauren smiled at me through her tears. I smiled back, holding in my emotions. I told her, "You know, Lauren, when I went away to school, I was only able to call my parents once a week. It was expensive and I had to get in line to use the phone, which was in the hallway of the dorm. You are only a cell phone call or an instant message away." I then kissed her good-bye. As I turned away from her and walked out the door, tears rolled down my cheeks.

During the return trip home, I had a lot of time to think—about Lauren, who I was leaving behind as she embarked on a new phase of her life, and about Sprite, who was entering his final phase of life.

I wondered if Lauren would ever see Sprite again. If she didn't, she would be devastated.

One thing I knew for sure: The next few months were going to be agonizingly tough.

EIGHT

A Hard Fall

September 2006

I was scheduled to attend a big radio semi-
nar in Dallas in the third week of September.
It was also my birthday. I don't mind these

conferences. They're usually twice a year. Although I'd rather stay home, you can't succeed at syndicating a radio show if you don't spend some time with the people who make your syndication possible, including program directors, station managers, broadcast executives, and trade media. As in other professions, these events allow you to meet and get to know many of them. But all I could think of was Sprite.

When I returned home, Sprite's condition had deteriorated badly. In a matter of days, he couldn't walk very well and even had difficulty standing. And when he did stand, his hind legs would shake. We had to carry him up and down the stairs. His sneezing, which was becoming more frequent, was almost violent. His jaw was becoming slightly unaligned as the right side of his mouth was more paralyzed than before. And his poor head looked worse than ever. I thought to myself, How could this be happening so fast? I'm not ready to lose my Spritey!

For the next several days we had a flurry of contacts and visits with the vets. We tried some new medicines. We tried adjusting his old medicines. We were just desperate to do whatever we could to stop his decline. But the prognosis wasn't good. The doctors couldn't have been kinder and more helpful, but they're not magicians. They can only do so much. They assured us that Sprite wasn't suffering, but there was no doubt he was struggling. They said we'd know when the time had arrived to let Sprite go. So we tried to keep him as comfortable as possible, and we gave him as much love and attention as there was time in the day.

Neither Kendall nor I could accept that we were losing Spritey. Neither of us had been through this before. Yes, we had had dogs, but we never had to make the final decisions about when or how to end their lives. This was taking a heavy emotional toll on both of us. I told Kendall that we needed to start thinking about how we would end Sprite's life if the quality spiraled downward and what we would do with his remains. But neither of us could bear to finish the discussion.

Some might say that we had plenty of time to prepare for this day. Maybe so, but it didn't make it any easier for my family or me. I remember reading a phrase somewhere: "No time on earth is long enough to share with those we love or to prepare our hearts for good-bye." I typed out that sentence and taped it to the top of my computer screen, where it remains to this day.

Chase could also see what was happening to Sprite. He, too, was spending a lot of time sitting with Sprite, petting him, and talking to him. I knew Chase was upset, but he mostly kept his emotions to himself. I let him know that if he wanted to talk, Kendall and I were there for him.

Lauren was still at college. She was coming home in a few weeks so Kendall and I decided not to tell her about Sprite's condition. There was no reason to upset her, especially since we wouldn't be able to comfort her as she was so far away.

Even Pepsi was concerned for his buddy. Pepsi is one of the most intelligent dogs I have ever seen. He's also a very perceptive dog. He can sense when something is wrong, and Pepsi knew that Sprite was in trouble. Pepsi is also a very happy and vibrant dog, but now there were times when Pepsi's tail and ears were lowered as he walked near Sprite. And he smiled much less when he lay down near Sprite. Pepsi knew. He would look at us as if asking, "What is wrong with Sprite?"

There were nights, when I was alone

working in my home office, that I could barely stand the emotional pain from the thought of losing Sprite. I had a very deep bond with this dog. He had suffered from a variety of ailments since the day we adopted him. And yet, Sprite was a dog at peace with himself. He didn't have a mean bone in his body. From the day we first met him at the foster parents' house, we were all taken by his friendliness and tenderness.

Sprite had overcome obstacle after obstacle. Now he was facing his biggest challenge and I felt I was letting him down. I was his caregiver, and in his time of greatest need I couldn't do a damn thing to help him. It was killing me.

I began reaching out to certain family members and close friends. One such friend was Rush Limbaugh. We have been friends for over fourteen years. All politics aside, he is one of the most compassionate and decent people I've known.

When I had complications from my heart surgery back in 2000 and spent nearly six months in and out of hospitals, Rush asked me what I needed to get well. I told him I was thinking of going to the Cleveland Clinic. He asked me why I didn't just go. I told him that

I had to find out if my insurance company would pay for the examination and procedures, which could be expensive. Rush responded, "The hell with the insurance. I'll pay for it. Just go, do whatever you have to do, and let me know how much it is."

As it turned out, I didn't need his help. My insurance paid for most of it, and I paid what remained. But I never forgot Rush's generous offer. And he is generous with complete strangers, too. But he doesn't like to talk about it, so I won't, either.

On September 29, 2006, Rush and I were instant messaging each other, as we do most nights. I rarely speak to him on the telephone. He is totally deaf and even with his cochlear implant he has difficulty hearing phone conversations. Since we're both on the computer most nights, instant messaging is the best way to communicate anyway.

But on this night, I was very down. As I was sitting at my desk, I could feel myself sinking into a dark hole. Rush and I talk about everything, so I began a conversation about Sprite and wore my emotions on my sleeve.

"Looks like our dog Sprite is dying," I started out. "I can't imagine dealing with this.

I pray I am wrong about this. May I ask you a question? When your cat was dying, what did you do?"

"I feel for you," Rush wrote. "Very sad when one of my cats died. She had a stroke. It was sudden. Gave her a weekend to recover then put her down. Very sad."

"Did you take her to the vet to be cremated?" I asked.

"Yes. Scattered her remains on the property."

"Been a long time since I really bawled, but won't be able to control it well here," I wrote. "This is going to freak you out. I've been wondering what the hell I am doing with my life sometimes. You ever do that? I just wonder sometimes if I should be doing something else. I always try to do the right thing, I try to be a good dad and husband, try to be a good friend, but just wonder about life's purpose."

Rush replied, "I once said that to a soldier I met at National Review's 50th Anniversary dinner. He lost an eye and an arm in Iraq. I felt embarrassed because he was praising me for my role. He pooh-poohed me and said, 'We all have our roles.' I think you have creeping guilt, Mark. Fight that. We are all who we are. It takes all of us to make a country."

I wrote, "People who are true believers in their particular religions have some satisfaction in that they think they know how things work. I don't know."

"I think about this all the time," Rush wrote. "I have incredible faith. I don't go to church but communicate with God so many times a day I can't count it. I know what you mean. You should research Malcolm Muggeridge. He sought to disprove Christianity and became a devout believer. I don't mean you should convert, just saying that smart people go through these gyrations all the time."

"Well, these dogs are the essence of love," I responded.

"Try to think of it this way," Rush wrote. "Your dog is a dog, an animal, unable to fend for itself because it is domesticated, etc. You took it in, gave it a life FAR better than it could have had on its own in the wild. Your dog Sprite has been loved and—in the case of dogs—knows it. And he loves you back, in his own way. Unconditionally. You have done a great thing by giving him the life he has had, and vice versa. It is all positive. Every living creature will die sometime. But the quality of life you have given Sprite has no doubt been much more than some humans have."

"Yes, I am trying to look at the bright side," I answered.

"If you are right and he is fading, you will miss him," Rush went on. "That is a sign of close attachment. But you can be assured that he had a great life for a dog. It was fulfilling both ways. And having him not suffer at the end is an act of compassion. It isn't easy emotionally and it shouldn't be because of the attachment. You get close to anything, you will eventually lose it, in one way or another. But it is the getting close that provides the joy. And it is worth it all in the end."

"Sorry to be a downer," I wrote.

"You are not a downer, Mark. This is deep stuff. It touches our souls. These are the things that give real meaning to life, which is what you are questioning tonight."

Then Rush added, "You never stop to think of all the amazingly positive ways you impact others for the good. None of us are aware of the positive ways we affect those we will never meet, but it is profound. You may think from time to time that your kids are in trouble, but they aren't. They are going through the normal stages at their time of life. Your influence/impact as a parent will blossom in them as human beings long after you are gone. And they will pass that on in the same way. It is an amazing cycle to me. You don't even stop to think about these things. But the way you feel about your dog is noticed by your children. It affects them in ways you cannot know and will translate in positive ways about how they treat other people and life in general. They are little things that continue to accumulate. Your values are what they are and they are good and they do get transferred."

"In the end," I wrote, "I don't deal with death very well. Funny, I'm not afraid of my own death, but worry about others close to me."

"I ponder this stuff all the time," Rush responded. "I know there are questions we humans are capable of asking to which there are no human answers, which proves the existence of God to me. That is natural, too, because you don't miss yourself when you die, but you will miss those you have loved and who die before you."

Rush continued, "You know what I have noticed? NOT ONE old person who knows they are going to die is ever panicked over it. Neither of my parents was panicked over it. There is something that happens. Sudden death, plane crash, whatever, is different. I've been thinking about it all my life. We all want to know the 'purpose' of all this."

"Well, Rush, I am going upstairs now to spend a little time with the dogs and then go to bed. You are a good friend."

"You, too, Mark, and enjoy your time with the dogs. Make the most of it, for yourself."

That's the Rush I know. The *real* Rush.

Sean Hannity is another dear friend. We also talk several times a day, including many nights when he's driving home from the Fox News Channel studios after *Hannity & Colmes.*

Sean has a thirteen-year-old dog named Snowball. Although she had not been experiencing any major illnesses, Sean told me she was slowing down. Sean bought her soon after he married his wife, Jill. He's very attached to Snowball and has been worrying about her health. When I commiserated with Sean about Sprite's failing condition, he understood what I was experiencing. He would try to ease my pain as best as anyone could by emphasizing how we had rescued Sprite.

"You probably lengthened Sprite's life by giving him the best medical care you could,"

Sean said. "Sprite knows he is loved and an essential part of your family."

Sean is very kindhearted and loyal. I could also tell that in trying to lessen my anguish, he was also dealing with his own feelings about Snowball.

For those of us who have older dogs, it's a continuous mental exercise to block the inevitable end of the relationship from your daily emotional palette. You try to appreciate the joy and love of the present. But the grieving process is anticipatory and begins as your dog shows signs of decline, no matter your best efforts to fight it.

My old friend Eric came to my house to help me with my computer. I don't know what it is about computers and me, but I have the worst luck with them. I had just purchased a new computer, which died within a week. I was having problems with the new replacement. Eric is a bit of a computer whiz, and he was lending me a hand.

Eric and I live within a few miles of each other. He had seen Sprite many times since the day we first brought him home. He has also known Pepsi since he was a puppy. When Eric came to the house this time, he was shocked at Sprite's appearance. I could hear it in his voice. He loved my dogs. Even so, he tried to lift my spirits. No one outside my immediate family can read my mental and physical state by looking at my eyes better than Eric. He knew I was upset.

Eric and I have experienced much together. I've known him since fifth grade. When we were growing up in Cheltenham Township, a suburb of Philadelphia, we would go to 76ers games, take the train into the city and spend hours at Independence Hall in Philadelphia (we both love American history), and work in political campaigns. When I was nineteen years old, I ran for the local school board with the help of Eric and my family. We knocked on thousands of doors. And I actually won!

Eric's mother was stricken with emphysema when he was only fifteen years old. She had been a chain-smoker for many years. She raised Eric by herself and he was her only child. Eric had to grow up fast when his mom got sick. I watched how he helped lovingly care for his mom, including fighting the bureaucracy to get her the medical equipment and treatment she needed. His mom struggled with that awful disease for several years. In her last year, she spent many days in the hospital.

One night, as I was visiting them at the hospital, she nearly died. I'll never forget it. The doctors and nurses had surrounded her bed and were working feverishly to revive her. They succeeded, but she passed away a few days later. Eric was only twenty-one. I remember his mom once thanked me for accepting him into our family. But it is I who am thankful for Eric. And I know his mom would be thrilled that we work together as colleagues each day in the same office.

Today Eric has three dogs. The eldest, Afton, is fifteen years old. He's also beginning to show his age. As Eric looked at Sprite, and then spoke to him and held him, I could see his genuine concern for Sprite. And I knew, as with Sean, he had to be thinking about his Afton and coping with his final days.

But I was still struggling with my emotions. My talks with Kendall and my friends weren't enough. I simply could not get my head around what was happening. To put it bluntly and honestly, I could not accept that God was treating my Spritey this way. Sprite had never hurt anyone. He had spent his life giving everyone around him love, affection, and happiness. He was kinder and gentler than most human beings despite all he had been put through. And now, having lived with us for only a few years, finally receiving the love, attention, and security that he deserved, he was dying. I could not understand how God could do this. I knew what the great religions, including my own, said about God's will, but none of it mattered. And I knew I wasn't the first to question it. I had also lost people and animals I loved before, but this was different.

As September ended and October began, something remarkable happened. About one week into the new month, Sprite started to rebound. He was a fighter, and he still wanted to live. He grew steadier and more active. I was thrilled one day when I took him for a walk, unhooked the leash from his collar, and he actually had the energy to make a "devil" run to the garage door like the good old days! I stood there for a moment, watching this magnificent event, and it was all I could do to stop myself from crying with joy.

It was a great day. It was as if Sprite gathered the energy so he'd be in better shape to see Lauren, who was coming home for a long weekend.

That weekend was a godsend. The family was together. I knew Lauren would soon be heading back to school. She spent a lot of time with Sprite—holding and talking to him. She also took several photos of him and them together. I treasured every moment.

It was a very important weekend for the Levin family.

Lauren would never see Sprite again.

NINE

Thanksgiving Prayers

November 2006

Sprite was feeling well enough for his grooming, so Kendall loaded Pepsi and

Sprite into the car and took them to the local groomer. She wanted them looking handsome for the holidays. The groomers understood Sprite's aches and pains and were gentle with him.

The dogs always looked so beautiful when they came home, and I always got the impression they knew it. Pepsi would race around the house. And even Sprite would walk from family member to family member, just to make sure everyone could see him. The groomers would put bandannas on them, which was a great touch, but I would always cut them off after about an hour so they wouldn't be bothered by them.

Our third Halloween with Sprite went well, unlike our first. Pepsi and Sprite were happily moving around the house with their tails wagging as they barked at the seemingly endless parade of trick-or-treaters. I looked over at them often. These days I was cherishing every moment with them, but also dreading that they might be our last with Sprite. I'd take whatever time we had together. All that mattered was that Sprite and Pepsi were happy.

November was a bad month for traveling. The prior spring I had agreed to make two business trips, which I could not cancel. And the prior summer we had made a significant deposit for a short trip to the Bahamas for Thanksgiving.

My first business trip was in early November, to visit my great local radio affiliate, WISN in Milwaukee. I left Virginia on Friday, November 3, returning the next day. I was busy at home the rest of the weekend and into the early part of the following week, monitoring the midterm election activities in preparation for my show.

Although I'm a political junkie, for the first time in thirty-five years my heart wasn't in it. It was a very important election, and I covered it as best I could. Of course I wanted my guys to win, but my passion was now focused on Sprite and the family.

I began to delude myself into believing that Sprite was recovering. He was looking and acting better. We were back to many of our routines. Pepsi and Sprite were hanging outside the door again, waiting for my radio show to end. They were joining me for dinner every night. Sprite was walking up and down the stairs better. And we were taking longer walks in the mornings and nights. But, of course, I was fooling myself.

One day in mid-November, Kendall and I noticed that Sprite was walking from room to room and then in circles. He wasn't doing it all the time, but enough to distress us. Also, when I would walk him, he started veering slightly to the right. Sprite's seizures, which had been limited and occurred mostly at night, had also become more frequent and lengthy. We were staying close to the house now, not wanting to leave him for long.

By now, Dr. Chris Hussion, who we had talked to so often about Sprite over the last several months, had become our friend. We asked Chris what was going on. He felt the tumor was expanding in Sprite's head and putting more pressure on his nerves, so Sprite was having difficulty controlling his movements.

We knew that damn tumor was the culprit, but we just didn't want to believe it. My heart sank. There was no way to reverse the growth of this tumor. It could only get worse. I asked Chris if he thought Sprite was in pain. He said he didn't think so. He likened the situation to human beings who've lost control over some of their body movements but still live on. Once again, we tried different medicines and combinations of medicines, but nothing worked.

Our poor dogs have no way to tell us what's wrong with them, how they're feeling, what they want us to do for them. Try as we may to figure out what they're going through and whether we are making the right decisions for them, we can never know for sure. That is part of the heartache that we humans must endure in our relationships with our dogs.

I now had to take a second business trip. This time, I went to Palm Beach, Florida, to attend the Restoration Weekend, a conference at which I had agreed to participate on a panel discussion about the judiciary. I thought about canceling at the last minute, but they were relying on me and I felt it would be dishonorable. The programs had been printed and much had been made of my attending. It was a four-day event. I spent the first day at the conference. I called Kendall from the hotel and asked her how Sprite was doing. She said not well. He was walking in circles more frequently. There I was, at the five-star Breakers Hotel, staying in lavish accommodations, surrounded by a beautiful view of the beach, hating every minute of it. I was in the wrong place at the wrong time.

I spent a second day in Florida, then I decided to visit my parents, who live in the nearby town of Boynton Beach. My mom and dad are up in years and neither of them is in good health. I hadn't seen them in a long while, even though my dad and I talk by telephone for a few minutes after every radio show.

My mom surprised me by preparing a delicious pre-Thanksgiving dinner. It reminded me of the great meals she made when I was a kid. Today she suffers from numerous medical problems, including heart disease and diabetes, and can barely walk or hear. But still, she went to all the trouble to make me that meal—turkey, stuffing, and lots more.

I was also very concerned when I saw my dad. He was thin and frail from recent surgical procedures. I knew he'd been through a lot the past few months, but I hadn't realized the toll it had taken on him.

I needed to be with my parents, even if only for a few hours, and they wanted to see me. My parents and I are very close. Everything I am and have achieved is due to what they've taught me, both by example and explanation. They have always encouraged me in all my pursuits. They have always worked hard. And they always sacrificed for my two brothers and me. My parents have unassailable integrity and character. They are devoted to each other and their family. They're responsible for instilling in me a love of God, country, and family.

Although I decided not to talk much with them about Sprite, just being around them and enjoying their company helped me immeasurably as I prepared to return home that night.

As I was coming home on Saturday, Kendall was leaving for the University of Alabama on Sunday. She was picking up Lauren and heading for the Bahamas, where Chase and I would later join them. This was to be a special Thanksgiving, but neither Kendall nor I wanted to go. We felt terrible about leaving, but we didn't want to disappoint the kids. Besides, I had dipped deep into our savings to pay for flights and our rooms at the Atlantis Resort. There was no way out.

It was all the more difficult because that Sunday night, I could see that Sprite had deteriorated further in just a few days. He was pacing the bedroom for the longest time. I sat with him on the floor, holding him in my lap to try to settle him down. He had become thin; he was losing muscle. I could feel his rib cage and shoulder blades. I spoke to him in a soft voice, telling him over and over again that I was with him, everything would be fine, and he needed to relax. I remember thinking for a split second that maybe this was just an episode or phase he was going through. But it wasn't. After a while, he struggled to get loose from me so he could pace again. Chris was right. He was walking in circles and around the room to the point of exhaustion not because he wanted to, but because he couldn't stop himself.

I put Sprite on the bed with me, which seemed to give him some temporary relief. He leaned his head against my leg and finally fell asleep. I dared not move for fear of waking him. But I couldn't take my eyes off him. I looked over every inch of his body— from his little white tail, worn paws and legs, his white, fluffy chest to his curly tan back, his mouth and head, and his resting eyes. I stroked his head, which that wretched tumor had misshaped, petted his thighs, and lifted his soft ears. I would do this often in the days ahead.

I realize now that I was using all my senses to forever imprint Spritey's life onto mine.

I saw that Pepsi was emotionally affected by Sprite's poor health, as well. That night Pepsi seemed a little scared and somewhat lethargic. He didn't understand what was happening to his friend, only that Sprite wasn't acting like his normal self. So Pepsi needed extra attention. I spoke to him and told him, "Sprite isn't feeling well and I don't know how much longer we have with him." I could tell by the way Pepsi looked at me that he knew.

The next day I decided that I would do everything I could to make sure that for the three days the family would be away, Sprite and Pepsi would get the best care possible and lots of attention by people who loved them.

I asked Chris if he would be willing to come to the house to check the dogs and make sure Sprite was as comfortable as possible. He agreed without hesitation. Chris is a very unique vet and human being. He truly cares for his animal patients and their owners, as do all the vets in this particular practice. He also took a special liking to Sprite and Pepsi.

We asked our neighbors the Mendoncas if they'd feed and walk the dogs in our absence. I warned them that this time it was different—Sprite wasn't feeling well and it would be a lot more work. The dogs would have to be walked at least four times a day, as Sprite was starting to have some accidents in the house. They were more than happy to help.

Eric offered to come to the house over the weekend to play with the dogs when he heard we were leaving town. And Lauren's boyfriend, Dan, played with them, as well.

I also prepared an extensive list to make sure each dog received the right food (Sprite was now eating soft food) and medicine, that certain lights would be kept on in the house to make sure Sprite could see where he was going, and the phone numbers where we could be reached.

I knew Sprite and Pepsi would be in the best of hands. And I was so thankful for these wonderful friends. But I still didn't feel

right. I was full of anxiety about leaving
Sprite.

On my broadcast on November 21, which
was the evening before Chase and I were to
leave town to meet up with Kendall and Lauren, I unexpectedly began sharing some
thoughts about Sprite, Pepsi, and Thanksgiving with my audience. It was my last
broadcast for several days.

I am very open and honest with my audience. Sprite and Pepsi were in my office as I
was on the air. As I looked at them, the
words and emotions just started to flow as I
spoke, at times with my voice breaking up:

**I want to talk about Thanksgiving for
a minute. We'll get to more news—
Lebanon and all of the rest of it. But it
really is important to take stock of the
people around you, to take stock of
what you have, what a great nation we
are. I know I do.**

**Thanksgiving is a very, very spe-
cial time. And I said in the first hour
that I have my dogs with me in the
studio tonight. We have a dog named**

Pepsi and a dog named Sprite. Pepsi's the dark dog. Sprite's the light dog.

Well, we adopted Sprite a little over two years ago from the humane society. Beautiful dog. Both males. Pepsi we got as a pup. He's about eight years old. Sprite—we don't know how old he is—but he's old.

And at the time we adopted Sprite they said he was three to six years old. The vet tells me he's at least twelve or thirteen years old. My guess is he's even older—and he's going downhill fast.

He's a wonderful dog. You people who have dogs know what I'm talking about. And just a terrific personality. Sweet as can be.

And he was diagnosed with a tumor in his head, oh, about eight, nine months ago. It's not malignant, doesn't cause him pain, but it causes certain disabilities. And I would give anything, anything for this dog to live another two or three months. Anything. But it's not going to happen.

So, as I sit here and I look at his

face, I give thanks for the fact that this dog came into our lives. People have lost a lot worse, I know that. Greg [Garvey], John [Wrobleski], others have lost sons in this war, daughters. People ravaged with cancer. Little children. My buddy, Mark Rypien, lost his son to brain cancer. I know it's all horrible.

But in any event, I give thanks to the good Lord for having even a short time with this dog.

What are ya doing there, Sprite? Come here. You just messed up my second-hour papers there, kiddo. That's okay.

Anyway, I don't know why I decided to share this with you. I share everything with you, my beloved audience. And I appreciate your loyalty. And I know many who are listening tonight are suffering horribly. They're suffering horribly by a loss of a loved one or a loved one who's suffering from a disease or they themselves are suffering from diseases.

They're suffering from some crime that's been committed against them or a member of their family. Or they're suffering from the fact that their loved one joined the military and is now suffering from a casualty or has perished. I know that. I know it.

And then there are those who are also suffering from the loss of a pet.

I often think about life and death, not in a morbid way. But you just wonder. You look at the dark sky and the clouds. On a clear night you look at the stars and you wonder. You wonder.

Thanksgiving is very, very important. And it's certainly important in the Levin household.

It wasn't my most articulate moment, but I said what I was feeling. And it was important, at least to me.

And as it turned out, to many who heard it.

On my fan website, marklevinfan.com, and another favorite website, freerepublic.com, several kind people in the audience posted comments after hearing my broadcast. I then realized how many people have had to go through the kind of grieving I was already experiencing. And let me tell you, it helps to know that you're not alone in this. There were a few posts that were particularly poignant.

Mark Dean:

I've lost grandfolks, uncles, and aunts. I've lost friends. I've lost a father. The death of a loved one is damn hard, no matter how, when, or why, and no platitude can minimize the pain and the lack we feel when they leave us. I've lost two dogs, too; one, my childhood pal, who escorted me into young adulthood, and the little mutt my wife and I rescued, who left us almost six years ago. We still have a ten-year-old puppy now. I will not attempt to compare the loss of a human life and that of a pet, except to say this: I handled the human loss much more bravely than I did the animal. You somehow steel yourself for the human loss you know will inevitably come, even if it is untimely and premature, but even though that goes triple for the animal loss (we all know anything over thirteen years is a gift), the loss and the lack somehow always sneaks in under the emotional radar and smart-bomb-slams your heart like you thought could never happen again. Perhaps it's the purity of the earnest unconditional love, loyalty, and devotion they give us that touches the core of our humanity, but all I know is that when my pups passed on, I cried like a baby and still choke back the tears when I recall it.

My favorite and somehow most comforting story on the subject is one I heard on some TV show about dogs that recounted an old American Indian legend that goes something like this: "In ancient times, when man and animals communicated as equals, a crack in the earth erupted. Man was on one side and the animals were on the other. The crevice grew wider and wider separating them and just before it became too large to traverse, the dog alone jumped over the chasm so that he could stay with man."

God bless Sprite, Mark. He'll be there waiting for you with big wet kisses as all our best friends will when we finally get to heaven.

Long Island Pete:

I can't tell you how much it saddened me to hear about your beloved pooch, Sprite. Being an owner of many dogs throughout my life, I know exactly what you are going through. They come into our lives and bring us such joy and happiness. When we have a bad day at work, we walk through the front doors of our homes and they are there to greet us, tail wagging and butt shaking. All of a sudden that bad day doesn't mean anything. And what do they want in return for the happiness they bring us? Love, unconditional love. A head to be scratched, a tummy to be rubbed, a ball to be thrown, or a place on the couch. Not too much to be asked from a loyal friend. A loyal family member.

It really hurts to see a loyal friend's days come to an end, but in the end that loyal friend knows he has been loved. He knows he had a good home and good people to take care of him. We wish he could talk and tell us what is hurting him and yet in a way they do. You can see it in their eyes.

If the good Lord doesn't take your dog home and the vet says to stick it out a little while longer because he isn't in pain, then that is what you do. Because in the end he will let you know when it is time. I have seen it happen many times. They know when the time is right for them to rest.

God bless you, Mark, and your family. You will be in my thoughts and prayers through this difficult time. Enjoy the holiday season as best you can and remember, you made a special pooch very happy in the time he was with you.

Havok:

Sorry for your loss. I, too, lost my friend Storm (ten-year-old Doberman) who was like my shadow, following me any and everywhere I walked.

We look back at the joy they brought us . . . but we do need to also know and feel good about the joy we brought them. Being a responsible, loving owner of a pet is a great thing, and that made our pets' lives complete and filled with love.

Saxmachine:

Seven years ago, my shepherd/Lab mix "Hooter" died in my arms on the way to the vet. For the most of us, our pets are family; they love us unconditionally, they know when we hurt and would do anything to ease that hurt. When Suzi moved into my house with her cat, Otto, he and Hooter hit it off right away. Otto had probably never seen a dog before so he didn't know he was supposed to be afraid. Hooter had lived with cats before so he saw a new playmate. They were buddies for six months. I think they both benefited. Our prayers are with you and your family as they always are.

Tiredoflaundry:

I lost my Porkie last year. She was twelve, and a special friend. She was not well, and I prayed to St. Francis to take her in her sleep. I was granted that blessing. I miss her something awful.

Task:

A little over five years ago a tearful doctor was in the process of euthanizing a doleful and nervous three-year-old Dachshund because of several intervertebral lumbar-disc events resulting in compromised and incomplete function of both back legs. A cursory exam revealed that although he had mobility problems he still had good superficial reflexes and his long-term prognosis might very well be okay provided that he was given the necessary care. It was at that point that I made the decision to assume the responsibility for the little dog's future. It is a decision that I am so very thankful I made. Elmo lived an additional five years and it was with great difficulty that I made the decision to end his life after determining by CT scan that the brain tumor that had so compromised his personality and happiness for the past three months had finally tipped the scale in a way that even the most abundant medical care, love, and attention that my wife and I could provide was insufficient to compensate for his discomfort.

I cannot say why this dog, of all the dogs that I have owned, and all the dogs that I have seen in the thirty-five years that I have practiced veterinary medicine and surgery, was the most cherished and most loved. Indeed, he was the most unique dog that I have ever known and he will never be able to be replaced.

I always try to be the best possible friend that I can be, yet I pale in comparison to what I have seen in canine counterparts, and Elmo was the tops.

Perhaps some day the souls of those who mean so much to each other will once again be united. Suffice it to say that I would rather be anywhere with those I love and care about than in heaven without them.

There were many more moving stories and good wishes from so many special people who are in my audience. I consider them part of my larger family. And just as I had the need to share a part of my life with them, they needed to do the same with me. It's not that "misery loves company," as the old saying goes, but that those in misery *need* company. They need to know they're not alone and that others who've gone through the same thing managed to survive it, despite their broken hearts.

TEN

A Desperate Search

December 2006

Kendall and I tried to make the best of our "vacation," but we were miserable. Despite all the planning and reservations, the hotel got our room assignment wrong. And since the place was packed for Thanksgiving, we had to move twice. The weather didn't cooperate, either. It was quite windy, and we didn't have one decent beach day. We tried to wear happy faces for the kids, but we were both emotionally spent. We were spending precious time in the Bahamas rather than at home with the dogs. Still, we tried to overcome a bad situation.

On the day after Thanksgiving, Lauren and I took a short taxi ride to Nassau. The taxi driver was probably the best entertainment and diversion on the island, a fount of island gossip. She couldn't have been more thrilled when I gave her a twenty-dollar tip, but she deserved it.

We walked through several shops, bought a few things, including a ring with a bright, multicolored stone, which I was going to give Lauren for Christmas. We went to the Hard Rock Cafe for lunch. The restaurant was located on a side street. We walked upstairs to the second floor and sat at a table outside on the patio. We could get a glimpse of the ocean, but mostly we looked down at the street and the people who were coming and going. Lauren and I talked about our beautiful surroundings and her return home from college in a few weeks. But it was surreal being in this place when I knew what must be going on back home.

Kendall and I decided we wouldn't tell her about the dire state of Sprite's condition. We didn't want her to grieve for weeks before she came home. But I didn't want Lauren to be totally in the dark. So I told Lauren that Sprite's health had taken a bad turn but that we were doing everything we could to help him. I also told her I didn't think he was on death's doorstep. When I said this to her, I half convinced myself because that's what I wanted to believe.

When we got back to the hotel, I called Chris to find out how Sprite was doing. He told me he had seen Sprite twice and Sprite was holding his own. He was eating and alert. Chris said he was pacing, but not too badly.

Saturday finally rolled around, time to leave. Lauren and Kendall had to take an earlier flight back to Alabama. Chase and I got to the airport four hours before our flight's departure, which wasn't a minute too soon. If you think our airports are a model of inefficiency, you've never tried to leave the

Bahamas. I was even pulled out of line by U.S. Customs for accurately reporting the value of the goods I was bringing back to the States. They were amazed at my openness and willingness to declare them as they were over the tax-exempt limit. The lines and waiting seemed to take forever. I was extremely anxious to get home to the dogs. We all were.

When Chase and I finally got home that Saturday, I wanted to believe that when we entered the house we'd see a healthier Sprite running with Pepsi to greet us as he'd done so many times in the past. Again, I was deluding myself. The dogs were happy to see us, but Sprite's condition obviously hadn't changed. When Kendall later spoke to Renata Mendonca, Renata politely suggested that Sprite couldn't last much longer. Renata told her they had to call Chris when we were away because Sprite hadn't been eating and he couldn't walk down the three steps through the garage for his walks. The Mendoncas loved Sprite and Pepsi. It was hard for them to go through this, too.

During the final days of November and early days of December, I worked mostly from home. I wanted to be around Sprite and

Pepsi. I knew these were Spritey's last days. It was time for us to make some of the decisions we had avoided for weeks. How would we end Sprite's life? What would we do with his body? I finally opened the desk drawer and took out that booklet from the vet's office. It compassionately discussed various end-of-life options, but I still could not find the strength to deal with it.

I could not look at Sprite and think about destroying him.

I decided to call my brother Rob. Many years earlier, Rob had to decide when and how to end his dog Tiger's life. Rob had had Tiger, who was half-black Lab and half terrier, for nearly fifteen years. Whenever I saw them, Tiger was by Rob's side. So I told Rob about Sprite's condition, and I asked him how he came to the decision to put Tiger to sleep and what he did with his body.

Rob told me, "Tiger's end came fairly quickly, over a period of about one month. He was having heart failure and fluid was building in his chest. The vet drained Tiger's chest but recommended putting him down." But Rob decided Tiger looked well enough and was fine mentally.

After he was away from home for a few

days, Rob returned and could see that Tiger's quality of life was poor. "He had stopped eating and drinking," Rob said. "I could see it was time. I called the vet and took Tiger to his office. Tiger lay in my lap until one of the rooms became available. It was extremely difficult, but I have no regrets. It would have been cruel to keep Tiger alive any longer.

"You know, Mark," he added, "there isn't a day I don't think about Tiger."

Rob had Tiger cremated. He keeps his ashes in a wooden box on a shelf. He also kept a piece of Tiger's fur.

I also spoke to my parents. Their dog Lady, a tiny black, brown, and white Chihuahua, lived over fifteen years. She was the third of their Chihuahuas. They told me that Lady had arthritis, a bad heart, and had been blind for many months. She also had kidney problems. My mother medicated her intravenously each day for a year, which prolonged her life. But she was getting sicker and sicker. My parents had scheduled to have her put to sleep. But on the morning of the day of the appointment, Lady stood up to go to the bathroom and fell over. My mother picked her up and Lady died in her arms.

Lady was cremated and my parents also have her ashes in a box on a shelf.

My talks with my parents and Rob—who had dealt with the same anguish I was experiencing—helped steady me for a few days. But it didn't last.

Kendall and I thought about burying Sprite, but community restrictions prevented us from burying his body on our property. I also tried to think of a way to ensure that somehow his life would go on, even if he wasn't with us in body anymore.

I spoke to a landscaper who was building a patio a few houses down and asked him if he could provide me with a small tree in the next week or so if I needed one. He said he could. I wasn't exactly sure what I wanted to do, but I thought about burying Sprite's ashes around a young tree on a special location in our yard.

I also went to Chris's office to look at the kind of box Sprite's remains would be placed in when they were returned to us. When he showed me a box, it was all I could do to contain my emotions. I didn't want to embarrass myself in front of his staff. In a broken voice, I said to Chris, "That looks so small."

He said, "Mark, most of our body is made of water." I thought, So this is what it comes down to. Ashes in a tiny box.

I asked Chris if Sprite's body would be treated with respect. He promised it would. He told me that the cremation company they use, which is in Pennsylvania, has the highest reputation and they had carefully checked them out before using them. I also asked him to make sure that Sprite's body was cremated by itself. He said he would. Beyond that, I said I didn't want to know anything else about the cremation process.

Preparing for Sprite's death was wearing on me. I wasn't sleeping, I was exhausted, and I was having difficulty concentrating on my work. I could feel my health deteriorating. My chest was often heavy and I was having episodes of angina.

My heart was breaking.

It was the first Saturday in December. Kendall and I knew it would be our last with Sprite. I went to the local supermarket to buy the dogs a brand of treats that I used to give them when we first adopted Sprite. I couldn't find them. I looked desperately at the rows and rows of food. They weren't there. I moved boxes and bags of dog food, peeking behind them in hopes of finding just one bag of the treats. Nothing. The grocery chain had stopped carrying them. We had plenty of other treats, but I had wanted to surprise Sprite and Pepsi.

I was emotionally down and sinking deeper and deeper. I thought it would help take my mind off Sprite for a short while if I went to the Dulles Town Center, a local mall where I could walk around and watch people happily going about their business. I stopped in a few stores, including Brookstone, which sells all kinds of gadgets. I didn't really look at anything. I was just kind of standing there. The manager, who was a fairly young guy, came up to me and said, "Mister, you don't look very happy. Maybe you should go get a drink and enjoy yourself."

"I don't drink," I told him, "but thanks."

As I continued to walk through the mall, I was looking for things that might make Sprite more comfortable. I came across Select Comfort, which sells mattresses made with some kind of airflow system. They were also selling an incredibly soft "micro" blanket. It was the perfect addition to the nest of my sweatshirts Sprite had been sleeping on. The salesman asked, "Who's the lucky person you're getting this for?"

"I'm getting it for my dog Sprite," I said.

"Lucky dog," he said.

"Not so lucky, really," I answered.

After about thirty minutes at the mall, I was ready to go home. It really hadn't helped. On the way out I passed a Jos. A. Bank clothing store. I'd been there before and bought a few things. The manager, Bob, was always outgoing and helpful. He usually had a couple of clever one-liners for me (and probably his other customers). This time, I noticed a pin on his lapel and I asked him what the pin stood for. "I'm a 9/11 family member," he said. "My brother died at the Pentagon."

Bob told me his brother was a civilian at the Pentagon who died when the terrorists crashed American Airlines Flight 77 into the building. My friend Barbara Olson was also on that flight. The captain of the airline was Charles F. "Chic" Burlingame, a brave man the terrorists murdered to gain control of the jet. Debra Burlingame, Captain Burlingame's sister, has become a close friend of mine.

I told Bob I was very sorry. He thanked

me. As I wandered the store aimlessly, Bob and I exchanged a few more pleasantries. I don't remember his exact words, but he made a joke about marriage. I saw he was wearing a wedding ring, so I asked him how long he had been married. He said, "I have been married for a few years. I lost my first wife to cancer."

I looked at Bob and thought, Here's a man who has every reason to be angry, to be an emotional wreck, to disengage from life, but here he is—pleasant to every stranger who walks into his store. He's still selling clothes, engaging in small talk, and smiling.

Bob had undoubtedly suffered terribly from the deaths of his brother and wife, but somehow he pulled through. Somehow he, like so many others in this world, was able to overcome unimaginable events and pain. I would think about Bob a lot in the weeks ahead. I still do. To me, he exemplifies the basic human desire to survive.

The next day, Sunday, I tried to keep myself busy. Shelves I had ordered for my garage from Lowe's had finally arrived. It wasn't exactly the most difficult home project I had ever undertaken. More than a year before I had paid my friend Rich to install the bracket system on which the shelves would be attached. I remember that day well because Sprite and Pepsi had a blast running around the house and barking at him.

But this day I didn't know what to do with myself. I was anxious and becoming distraught. That night, like most Sunday nights, I went to the Outback Steakhouse. I could barely choke down my dinner, so I left most of it uneaten. I tried to engage in polite talk with the people around me, but I couldn't. I ordered takeout for Kendall and Chase and returned home.

When night came, I knew it was Sprite's last Sunday. No more weekends together.

No more watching football in our TV room, where he would keep Pepsi and me company.

No more long Sunday-morning and -evening walks.

When the sun went down that night, it was as if a beautiful, bright shooting star had disappeared into the dark sky. And that star had symbolized Sprite's life.

It was time to ready myself for what would be a week of pure agony.

From that point forward, I remained at the house with Sprite and Pepsi.

On Monday I tried to mask my pain and do my radio show as best I could. I don't know if I was all that convincing. I had also contracted some kind of virus, which was causing me to cough and have shortness of breath. I sounded awful.

I decided my last broadcast for the week would be on Wednesday, December 6. So I asked Phil Boyce—vice president of news/talking programming at ABC, my close friend, and the person responsible for giving me my first break in radio—if I could take a few days off at the end of the week. He said of course. The Boyces, Hannitys, and Levins have spent several vacations together at Disney World. Phil knew of my attachment to my dogs, and he knew I was about to lose one of them.

My older brother, Doug, called me. He lives outside of Philadelphia. He offered to drive 170 miles to our house and help out any way he could. I told him thanks, but there was nothing he or anyone else could do. Doug always worries about my health.

I've always admired Doug's strength and sensitivity. When Doug was thirteen years old, he had major back and neck surgery to correct severe scoliosis. He was in a full body cast for four months. Afterward he wore a brace that went from his ears to his lower thighs for twenty-three hours a day over the next five years. And he never complained.

I hung up the phone and wished I had an ounce of his strength.

On Wednesday afternoon, December 6, as I sat in my basement office and prepared for my show, I decided to walk upstairs and see how the dogs were doing. It was also the day our housekeepers, Manuel and his assistant, were in the house. As I reached the top of the stairwell, there was a strange silence. I didn't see or hear the dogs. I happened to looked out the window near the front door and, to my disbelief, Pepsi was sitting outside on the front steps. I immediately thought to myself, Oh my God, Sprite must have followed him. Since the front door was locked, I ran to the garage door. The garage door was open and Sprite had wandered off!

I freaked out. I shouted to Manuel's assistant, "Where is Sprite?!" She speaks Spanish and doesn't understand English well. I unintentionally frightened her, which I regretted. I then ran outside and began to frantically search for him. I didn't know where to look first. Should I look along the river? Should I look in the woods? Should I go down the street? Kendall was miles away meeting with a friend. I called her on her cell phone and told her to hurry home. She was panicked, too.

I ran down to the river behind the house. I was repeatedly calling out Sprite's name. He was almost completely deaf, but what else could I do? There was so much area to cover. I couldn't search all of it. I cried out, "Oh, please, don't be in the river." Sprite was so weak there's no way he'd survive.

Minutes later, I decided to head for the woods, which are located on a very steep hill on the side of my house. I figured he might be there since they're closer to the house. I ran through the weeds and bushes, stumbling on tree roots and vines. The ground was thick with dead leaves that had fallen from the mass of trees. I had trouble keeping myself from sliding down the hill. All of ten minutes had passed, but it seemed like hours. I was out of shape. My heart was pounding. I had great difficulty breathing. And there was still no sign of Sprite.

I was getting more desperate. I knew every second counted. What was I going to do? I couldn't believe Sprite's life was going to end this way. He could barely stand up, let alone defend himself from foxes, raccoons, and other predators and scavengers who roam our neighborhood. And if I didn't find him before nightfall, he'd surely freeze to death—if he wasn't already dead.

I returned to my driveway. Manuel came up to me. He was upset that his assistant had been frightened. I assured him that I had not yelled at her, but had hollered in disbelief at Sprite's disappearance. He understood. He then helped me look for Sprite.

I returned to the woods. Across the way, on the other side of the hill, there were three men building a stone wall for another home. I called to them, "Have you seen my dog?! He's tan and white! I can't find him!"

They also spoke Spanish, but their English was good enough for me to hear one of them yell, "No, sir. . . . Wait. I see him. He's in the creek!" Sprite had apparently wandered about a block away and tumbled some sixty yards down the wooded hill into the creek. I couldn't imagine what shape he might be in.

One of the men across the way took off to get him. At the same time, Manuel and I quickly went down the hill and headed along the creek toward Sprite. They were much faster than I. I was still breathless. I had slid down the hill. By the time I managed to get up and start down the creek, they were out of sight. As I continued down the creek, Manuel appeared in the distance. He was cradling Sprite in his arms and working his way back up the hill. I shouted, "Is he okay?"

"I think he is," Manuel answered.

As Manuel carried him to the house, I was finally able to climb back up the hill. Manuel and I hugged each other. "I can't thank you enough," I said. "I am so grateful. God bless you." Manuel had a big smile on his face. Kendall then arrived and we all went in the house. Incredibly, Sprite had not been hurt. He was just muddy. It truly was a miracle.

I asked Manuel, "Do you think it's time?" He said, "Yes, Mr. Levin. I know how hard it is. I've had to do it." I knew he was right. I later learned from Kendall that Manuel is also a minister with his own congregation.

That night Sprite circled for hours, stopping only when he collapsed from exhaustion. Kendall and I decided tomorrow would be the day.

Sprite had been saved from a potentially awful death, only to die the next day.

ELEVEN

Good-bye My Beloved Sprite

December 7, 2006

December 6 was coming to an end. It was the night before the day Kendall and I decided we had to put Sprite to sleep. We broke the awful news to Chase. He was upset but very strong. I could see his eyes well up, but he held his emotions back.

Chase spent extra quality time with Sprite that night. He didn't go to bed until after the usual time. And before he did, he asked Kendall and me, "Can we wait one more day? I'd like more time with him." It was all I could do to control my emotions. I thought to myself, If we could only have one more day. Oh, do I wish.

We told Chase that Sprite was miserable and that we owed it to him to help him out now. He said he understood. I later went into his room and sat on his bed next to him and asked Chase if he was okay. He said he was, but I knew he wasn't. I told him mom and dad were there for him if he needed to talk.

There was no way to prepare for this day. We knew it was coming, but it didn't matter. It was still happening too fast. He was our baby. He had just started to enjoy life with a family that loved him and treated him with the care and affection he had deserved since he was a puppy. We wanted more time with Spritey. We needed more time with him.

We had only had him for twenty-six months. It wasn't long enough.

That night I did something I rarely do. I prayed. I prayed to God to take Sprite in his sleep. I begged Him.

"God, please take Sprite quietly and painlessly as he sleeps. Please take him in your arms in the middle of the night. He needs your help. We need your help."

When I woke up that morning, Sprite was sleeping on my sweatshirts. He looked so peaceful. His breathing was a bit labored, but his eyes were closed, he was on his side, and he seemed to have a smile on his face. Maybe it was my imagination.

The end came on December 7. Ironically, it was the sixty-fifth anniversary of the Japanese attack on Pearl Harbor. I hadn't realized it until later. I also learned the next day that former Ambassador to the United Nations Jeane Kirkpatrick had passed away that December 7. She had been a hero of mine.

But for the Levin family, it was to be our saddest day, the day we were losing our Spritey.

Around 7:45 A.M. I called Chris. I told him

that Kendall and I had decided today was the day. He told me we had made the right decision and it was the humane thing to do now. The soonest he could come to the house was between noon and 12:30 P.M.

I just set in motion the events that would end Sprite's life. The pain of that phone call was unbearable, but I had to keep myself together. Something kept me from calling Chris back and canceling the appointment. I struggled to keep the strength to follow through. I knew I must, for Sprite's sake, and for the rest of the family.

I drove Chase to school that morning, as I do most mornings. When I pulled up to the school to drop him off, I asked him if he was okay. He said he was. I held his hand and told him I loved him. I sat in the car and watched him walk into the school.

I was so proud of my son. This was one of the worst days of his young life, but he kept his chin up, went to school, and carried on.

He knew when he'd come home that afternoon, Sprite would be gone.

When I returned home, I spent more time with Sprite. He actually seemed more relaxed than in past weeks. I lay down next to him, looked into his eyes, and I cried. I told him I was sorry, that I loved him, and that there was nothing else I could do for him. I told him we would never forget him and that he was going to find some peace now. I thanked him for all the joy he had brought us and for making my life so much richer and happier. I told him I was sorry for all the health and physical problems he had to endure and if he had suffered as a result of anything I had done or failed to do.

Then I just looked at him. He was so weak and fragile. Whatever his age, now perhaps fifteen years old, he was finally showing it. And yet, he was still so beautiful and majestic. Once again I stroked his incredibly soft fur, especially his chest, which he always liked. I slowly petted his back. I held his paws and examined them for the last time. I gently massaged his thighs. I stroked his head and touched his ears with my fingers. And I kissed him. I kissed him a lot. I kissed his nose, his cheeks, and the top of his head.

Then I buried my face in his chest for a brief moment, as I had done so many times before. Sprite always smelled clean and fresh, and it was no different that day.

* * *

A little later I could see Kendall sitting on the floor with Sprite, holding him and talking to him. Kendall has a soft, kind voice. She was whispering good-bye to him, loving him, and reassuring him. Sprite and Kendall had a special relationship. But for Kendall's persistence, we would never have been blessed with this dog. Kendall had made all those trips to Maryland to find him and she had persuaded the foster parents to let us adopt him over another family. Kendall had worked with the humane society to finalize the paperwork. And Kendall had spent many hours with Sprite during those first days, taking him to the original Poolesville veterinarian to address a variety of minor health issues.

Sprite adored Kendall. He must have understood that she was responsible for bringing us all together. When Kendall walked in a room, Sprite never took his eyes off her. When she left a room, Sprite and Pepsi would be right behind her. Sprite knew that Kendall was his loving mother. He knew that she'd do anything for him if she could. They adored each other. But there was nothing she could do for him now. Kendall had saved him once, but she couldn't save him this time. Nothing could.

My cell phone rang. It was Jim Robinson, president of the ABC Radio Networks. He was calling to congratulate me on my radio ratings.

In a cracking voice, I said to Jim, "Within a few hours I am putting my dog Sprite to sleep. I would trade all my ratings and my career if I could keep my dog."

Jim paused and said, "I am so sorry. I know what you're going through. My family has several dogs, and we recently lost one. It's the worst feeling possible."

Jim also mentioned that Mitch Dolan, president of ABC Radio, who was a major impetus behind syndicating my show, had lost a dog a few weeks earlier in a tragic accident. I told Jim to please give Mitch my sincerest condolences; he could obviously tell I was upset from my shaky voice, so the conversation was short.

There were a few hours left until Chris would arrive. Kendall and I decided to take the dogs outside, where they'd be together for the last time. It was around 10:30 A.M. It was a chilly day, about forty to forty-five degrees. The sky was clear. As the sun shone on the dogs, the full extent of Sprite's weakened body became unmistakable. The arthritis had ravaged him. It had caused his back to become hunched and crooked. The loss of muscle mass had caused his ribs to become visible. Sprite could barely stand up, let alone walk, but he tried. He had a will to live that had carried through the last years of his life, and it was still there. Somehow, somewhere he found the energy to walk. He was unsteady. But he walked.

Kendall, Pepsi, and I took Sprite to his favorite spot in the backyard—a little hill on the corner of our property where you can look up the Potomac River. As we reached the spot, the breeze began to pick up. It had to be twenty to twenty-five miles per hour. Sprite stopped in his tracks, looked into the wind, and he appeared as content as I'd ever seen him.

Boy, did he love a good breeze.

And we were so lucky that there was a breeze that day. This would be the last time Sprite would go outside, the last time he'd inhale the outside smells and fresh air. It would be the last time he'd see the trees and bushes he'd become familiar with.

The last time he'd enjoy a breeze.

I picked Sprite up and held him in my arms. He nestled his head in the fold of my left arm. His ears were blowing back, as they always did in the wind. Together we looked upriver in the direction of the breeze—the same direction as the White's Ferry crossing. As I was holding Sprite, I thought about my trip on that ferry, when I went to see Sprite for the first time. I thought about all the times Kendall used it in those early days of our time with Sprite.

As I held Sprite closer to me, the breeze picked up. He looked so content. He seemed to be smiling again. At that moment, I wondered if God was calling Sprite and Sprite knew it. Maybe that's what I wanted to think.

We took a few final photos with the dogs. Unfortunately, the photos in which I was with the dogs didn't turn out. But we do have two with Kendall and the dogs, which I look at every day—over and over again.

Renata, our friend and neighbor who had lovingly cared for Sprite and Pepsi when we had to leave town, walked over to us. We gave her the sad news. She hugged each of us and quietly returned to her house. Her family adored the dogs and she would have to find a way to tell her kids why they wouldn't be seeing Sprite anymore.

We returned to the house. Kendall fed the

dogs. That's right. Sprite was hungry and thirsty. He hadn't lost his appetite. We also gave them some treats. I told Kendall to give Sprite his arthritis medicine. She looked at me and said, "Mark, Sprite doesn't need his medicine." You'd have thought that by this time I would have accepted that this was the end, but I hadn't. It struck me again, as if I'd received a body blow to the stomach, that this was it. There would be no tomorrow for Sprite.

As we waited for Chris to arrive, I said to Kendall, "This is like waiting for the Grim Reaper." We didn't know whether to hope for the time to move quickly or slowly. Kendall turned to me, with tears rolling down her checks, and said, "He's eating and drinking. He's having a good day. This is so awful." And it was.

Sprite had somehow rallied for us one last time. It was both magical and torturous.

We wanted to be with Sprite in his final moments. We wanted him to be in familiar surroundings. We had to pick a place in the house where Sprite's life would be ended— another difficult decision. We decided on one of his favorite resting spots in the family room. I arranged my sweatshirts and the new blanket in a nest. Sprite was circling the room, but not as much as in recent days. And in the last few minutes before Chris arrived, Sprite plopped down right on the spot. He seemed so comfortable. There he was, like a little dear, just resting there. I never told Kendall, but I had to fight every urge and instinct in my being not to call it off. I came very close to calling Chris and telling him to turn around, but I didn't. Somehow I went on with it.

Kendall and I lay down on the floor next to Sprite. We held him and spoke to him again. Pepsi was roaming around the room. He could tell something unusual was happening, or about to happen, but how could he understand the dire event that was to occur and that would end the life of his best furry friend?

I kept looking at my watch and then at Sprite. It was only a matter of minutes now. It was around 12:20 P.M. As I went over to the window, I saw Chris driving up to the house. I turned to Kendall and said, "He's here."

Chris came into the house through the garage. He was holding what appeared to be a small doctor's bag. He also had a heavy blanket under an arm. I knew what the blanket was for—to carry my Spritey away when the procedure was finished.

We leaned down around Sprite, who was still lying on his left side. Kendall looked into his eyes and was stroking his head. She was trying to smile through the tears that were pouring down her cheeks so Sprite would see her "happy" face during his final moments of life. I was sitting next to Sprite's hind quarters, stroking his back and legs. He lifted his head and sniffed my hand, making sure I was there with him and looking for reassurance.

Chris sat on the floor between Kendall and me. I said to him, "Promise me he won't feel anything." He said, "Mark, the first thing I am going to do is give him a sedative. That will relax him. It will take about five minutes to take effect. He won't feel a thing."

The next step would be administering an overdose of a barbiturate through an artery in Sprite's leg, which would stop Sprite's heart in twenty to thirty seconds.

Every day I relive the details of this heart-breaking procedure. But I will not describe them all, as Lauren and Chase were not there. I will say only that after about twenty seconds from the time the barbiturate had been administered, I asked Chris if Sprite had passed away, and he said that he had. I asked him to make sure. Chris checked Sprite with his stethoscope, looked at me, and ever so slightly nodded his head. I said quietly to Kendall, "He's gone," and I cried for a brief moment. Kendall put her hand on mine. She was sobbing. And for the last time I touched one of Spritey's legs, petted his side, and patted his head.

I then said good-bye for the last time. It was 12:30 P.M., and it was over.

I could barely speak, but managed to ask Chris to wrap Sprite in the new blanket I had bought him the weekend before, which he did. I thanked him for all his help. I wasn't able to say anything else. I wasn't able to watch him wrap Sprite in the blanket. I had to step away.

Kendall accompanied Chris to his car. She wanted to be with Sprite until the car drove off. I looked out the window. I saw the bundle in the blanket that was Sprite carefully held in Chris's arms. I then turned away for the final time.

*   *   *

My grief was overwhelming and immediate. Although the euthanizing process went as planned, and Sprite hadn't suffered, I was traumatized. Sprite was now gone, never to return. My heart was already aching, and Sprite's absence from the house was already apparent.

I also was racked with guilt. I felt I had just executed my dog. Each step of the procedure only enhanced that feeling. Sprite had sought my reassurance, which I used to betray him and trick him into remaining calm before the drugs were administered. Yes, I knew Sprite couldn't go on. Yes, I knew his condition would only get worse. Yes, I knew he had to be miserable and I was out of options. But I could not escape the fact that the dog we had taken home, who we loved and who loved us, who had been so happy and brought us so much joy was destroyed on my say-so. I had been responsible for deciding the day, time, and place of his death.

Who was I to make these decisions? Who was I to play God?

My guilt would only get worse.

TWELVE

Dark Days

December 2006

After Chris left with Sprite, I went to the living room and sat on the floor next to the sofa where Sprite would often rest and watch the front door. Pepsi was sitting with me. I began crying. It wasn't very loud, and it didn't last long, but it was intense. I hadn't cried like that since I was a young child. Kendall wasn't near so she didn't hear me, but Pepsi was. His ears and tail drooped, and he bowed his head.

I believe at that moment Pepsi realized that Sprite was gone and that he wasn't coming back.

As I walked around the house, I had an empty feeling. I was numb and directionless. Everywhere I looked I saw reminders of Sprite. His food and water bowls and his leashes were in the mudroom. Sprite's favorite blankets and sweatshirts were still located in his favorite nesting spots. Sprite shed a lot, so his fur was on the furniture and carpet. And Sprite's medicines were lined up on a shelf in the pantry. The labels read "Mark Levin's Sprite."

Kendall picked Chase up from school a few hours later. She told him that Sprite went to sleep and he didn't feel anything. She told him that it was a very hard decision, but he wasn't suffering anymore. Chase didn't say much. It was hard news for him, but he prefers to wrestle with his emotions privately, like many teenagers.

That evening, as I went on my computer to try to distract myself, I noticed an e-mail from Mitch Dolan. As president of ABC Radio, Mitch is a very busy man, and we rarely get to speak, so I figured his e-mail had something to do with my radio show.

I was wrong.

Mark:

Jim [Robinson] gave me the sad news about your pup. I'm so sorry you are going through this.

Two weeks ago our two golden retrievers, Lumpy and Cinnamon, chewed a hole in the fence (as they would frequently do) and took off. Usually they would wander home (covered in mud from the reservoir) or we would get a call after a few hours from someone in a nearby neighborhood or one of the adjacent towns, letting us know that our dogs were in their backyard playing with their kids and we'd just drive over and pick them up. My wife Fran called me in New York that afternoon to let me know that they had taken off again and obviously our expectation was that they would turn up, as they always had before. I got home that night around 10 PM—no dogs, no calls, and Fran had been driving around for hours. As we continued to search, our sense that something bad happened grew and, unfortunately, was confirmed earlier the next morning.

The Lewisboro Police (next town)

called and apparently Lumpy and Cinnamon had wandered into a neighbor's backyard (only about ¼ mile from our house, which we passed by about a dozen times the night before) and fallen through the cover of an ungated swimming pool. The neighbor indicated he didn't return home until 11:30 that night and didn't hear anything but saw the dogs the next morning, at which point he called the Lewisboro Fire Department. (The guy was waiting in his car for the fire department to pull the dogs out because "he had to go to work." The fire department called the police department and filed a complaint because of the broken gate, but what kind of human sees two dogs trapped in his pool and doesn't jump in and pull them out?)

Goldens are amazingly strong swimmers, but the water level had been lowered, the pool had no steps, the ladder was pulled out—and they simply couldn't get out. They were in the water all night and Lumpy (the older male) drowned—got tangled in the pool cover—but Cinnamon managed to somehow hang on. She was worn-out and misses her buddy terribly (as we do), but she's fine.

We've had a number of goldens over the years and I was always with them when the time came. I miss Lumpy terribly, but the thought that the last thing he saw was a vinyl tarp, instead of my face, will kill me forever.

It hurts unimaginably to say good-bye to a best pal, but balanced against the unconditional, unqualified love and devotion we receive for the time we have them, it may be the best and most inequitable deal known to man.

Sorry for the ramble, but my heart is breaking for you. I'll have a good thought for all Levins tonight.

Mitch

I wrote Mitch back telling him, "I feel terrible about your loss of Lumpy and the horrible ordeal. I cannot imagine the hole your family feels. I am so sorry. I am grateful for your kind note."

And then I added, "Dogs are the best. And as you say, their entire existence is to give us love and pleasure. They are selfless. I am truly sorry you had such a tragic experience with Lumpy. And I know how difficult it must have been for you to write about it. Lumpy will have a new friend now—my Sprite."

I realize some might say this is weird stuff—two grown men writing each other this way about their dogs. But those who would say that have *never* owned a dog. If they had, they'd understand.

There was a ring at the door. It was a man delivering a large bouquet of flowers. The accompanying card read "In Memory of Sprite—Sean and Jill Hannity."

Sean and I had spoken briefly earlier in the day. In a compassionate voice he said, "Mark, I know you're crushed. I hate seeing you like this. It's killing me. I feel terrible for you and the family." I told Sean I had to hang up before I lost my composure. Sean tried to reach me later in the day, but I was out of pocket—at home with Sprite in his final hours.

I called Sean and thanked him for the flowers. He told me that when I'm ready, he wanted to buy me another dog. I thanked him again and said, "Sean, I have Pepsi. He needs our full attention now. There won't be another dog in our house. This is way too painful."

Sean is such a thoughtful and generous friend. He truly would give me the shirt off his back if he thought I needed it. I am lucky to know him as I do.

I went back to my computer. Rush was online, so I started a conversation with him: "I am so tired, so emotionally spent," I wrote. "I really am beginning to question my career. I go back on the radio, talk and talk and talk. Meanwhile, life and death things are happening. My dog has died, people work all day at these humane societies—I don't know how they do it but I admire them. Vets have a purpose, doctors have a purpose, what the hell do I do—talk and talk and talk. I am distraught."

"Yes, I think you are in the throes of sadness because of Sprite," Rush responded. "As is the case with all of us, we are ignorant of the profound impact we have on the lives of others. You should watch the movie *It's a Wonderful Life*. Not kidding."

"I look at these innocent little lives," I answered, "who give us nothing but love, they are here for such a short time. They exist to give us pleasure, and they're gone the next day. I had this dog for two damn years. I couldn't have him for five?"

"Yes," Rush wrote, "and you never stop to think of the comfort and happiness you are providing these innocent little lives. Where would Sprite have been without you and your family? Sprite was a happy dog and he brought happiness to the family. Pets are the essence of innocence, like babies. We end up treating pets like our children. Pets are the only creatures who give humans uncon-ditional love. Your pet never yells at you, rejects you, tells you to go to hell or argues with you. They appear helpless and when they die you get angry you can't save them."

"Exactly right," I wrote. "But I think about those parents who've lost kids in car acci-dents and in war or to brain cancer—and look at me."

"Loss is loss," Rush replied. "Stop com-paring. Stop with the guilt. You will not suc-ceed trying to minimize your loss compared to the tragedies of others. You are beating yourself up for no reason. Your emotions are real and justified and you should not have guilt over them. What you did today was humane."

"But he's gone now, never to return, as we all are when our time comes," I wrote.

"Yes, Mark, but even Sprite leaves a legacy."

I wrote, "I have thought about writing a book about him, but nobody will care."

"Sprite no doubt taught you much—about the way he lived his life with the cards he was dealt and your family's genuine compassion to love him and help him," Rush wrote.

"Well, nobody would want to read about my dog," I answered.

"Sure they would," he wrote, "and your family's life with him. It would touch millions of hearts."

"I am lucky to have you there, Rush. If people only knew what a decent human being you are. Thank you."

Now you know where I got the initial encouragement to write about Sprite and Pepsi.

I had also remembered that Laura Ingraham had just lost her dog, Troy. I've known Laura since we both worked in the Reagan administration. I sent her an e-mail telling her about Sprite and asking her how she dealt with Troy's passing. She wrote:

I am so very sorry, Mark. It is absolutely the WORST thing. I ache every day and at the same time I still feel as though Troy is with me. One night I swore I heard him breathing in my room. Sprite was lucky to have you—you were the guardian angel in Sprite's life. You should always treasure knowing that you gave Sprite "stolen time." That is a testament to you.

It was really a testament to Kendall. She was the angel who rescued Sprite.

I later spoke to Laura. She had had Troy for fifteen years. He was a yellow Lab. Laura was still hurting. It had only been a few weeks since Troy had been put to sleep, but Laura couldn't have been more supportive.

Laura would later bring another pup into her life—another yellow Lab named Lucy.

As I took Pepsi for his walk late that night, I was reminded of Sprite when we passed all of his favorite bushes, trees, and posts. It was hard to take. For the next few days, when I walked Pepsi, I hoped I wouldn't come across any of the neighbors. I knew they'd ask me about Sprite, and I didn't want to answer. So I would wear my baseball cap and pull it low over my eyes.

One neighbor, whose name I don't know, was walking her dog toward us. I'd seen her several times before, and we'd exchange pleasantries. She noticed Pepsi and I were without Sprite. She asked, "Where's your other dog?" In a quiet voice I answered, "We had to put him to sleep." "Oh, I'm so sorry," she said. As I fought back the tears, I thanked her and moved on.

In the days ahead, more and more neighbors—especially the children—noticed that Sprite was gone. Sprite and Pepsi had been fixtures in the neighborhood. They were always together. A young teenage boy who lives down the street came up to me and wondered where Sprite was. I told him Sprite had been very sick and passed away. I could see on his face that he was saddened and embarrassed he had asked me. I told him, "It's okay. Sprite lived a long time and he was very ill at the end."

While I was able to comfort the young man, I was unable to find peace myself. Despite the extraordinary kindnesses of family and friends, I was still struggling. I didn't need a psychiatrist to tell me that for weeks leading up to Sprite's death, I had been depressed. But now it was getting worse. Kendall could tell I was in agony. While she, too, was upset, her deep faith helped her cope better. She felt such relief that Sprite was no longer miserable and, as Kendall put it, "was frolicking in doggy heaven."

Kendall later asked me if I needed to see someone to assist me with grieving. I told her no, I'd work through it. I had to.

As it happened, it would take months.

Over and over in my mind I would think about our twenty-six months with Sprite. It seemed like we had known him forever.

I thought about the first time I had laid my eyes on Sprite at the foster parents' home, and how he had won my heart from that very moment.

I thought about all the trips Kendall had made to Maryland to bring this precious dog into our lives.

I thought about that frightening Halloween night when Sprite collapsed and I rushed him to the animal hospital.

I thought about the walks along the river with Sprite and Pepsi.

I thought about the cute way in which Sprite would run and how he would draw attention to himself when he wanted a treat or to go outside.

I thought about the companionship Sprite brought Pepsi, and how the two quickly became inseparable.

I thought about all the times Sprite would lick Pepsi on the head, and how Pepsi learned to reciprocate.

I thought about all those late nights I kept Sprite company when he would bark at the light reflecting off the river from the water tower or the trees waving in the wind.

I thought about how excited Sprite would get during the holidays, birthdays, and when the kids' friends would come to the house.

I thought about Lauren's high school graduation party, when Sprite and Pepsi greeted the guests with big smiles on their faces and tails wagging—as they scouted the house looking for opportunities to get some food.

I thought about Sprite and Pepsi barking at the deliverymen, only to befriend them when they'd come through the door.

I thought about Kendall walking through the house with Pepsi and Sprite parading behind her.

I thought about all the times Sprite cuddled with us—how he'd lean against us, sit in our laps, and nuzzle us with his head.

I thought about all the times I held his head in my hands, looked him in the eyes, kissed him on his nose, and told him how much I loved him.

I thought about all those times we'd come home and Sprite and Pepsi would be ecstatic to see us.

I thought about Sprite and Pepsi sitting outside my office door, waiting patiently to join me for dinner after my radio show.

My sense of loss was overwhelming.

In the midst of all of this, I remembered that the day before Sprite passed away, my friend Debra Burlingame lost her niece Wendy in a terrible fire. Wendy was Chic Burlingame's daughter, one of the hero pilots murdered on 9/11. "How much tragedy must one family withstand?" I thought to myself.

I called Debra to give her my sympathies and see how she was doing. She told me about her niece Wendy and her brother Chic's adoration for her. She wanted Wendy's little girl to remember her mom and was already compiling an album for her.

Debra then observed, "Mark, you sound very sad to me. What's wrong?"

I was hesitant to discuss Sprite with Debra, only because her own loss was so recent. I also thought Debra would think I was nuts, considering the enormity of what she'd just been through. I told her about Sprite and his recent passing. She was inquisitive and wanted to know more. So I told Debra all about him.

Well, it turns out that Debra loves dogs, too. She understood the special bond.

Later that day, she sent me this e-mail—to cheer *me* up:

We take our relationship with our dogs very, very seriously.

Chic had two golden retrievers that he loved. Beautiful dogs. One day when he was doing yard work, the dogs were out there with him, loose, he looked up and they'd vanished. He was distraught. Not content to be passive about it, he printed up 1,000 flyers with a color photo of the dogs, offering a $1,000 reward. His strategy was to put them in so many places that whoever took the dogs (he was convinced they were swiped)

wouldn't be able to get away with it—too many people would be on the look-out for them. His strategy worked. A 10-year-old Cub Scout went looking for them and found them wandering around an area a few miles away. Chic told me that when he got the call, he hung up the phone and broke down crying. He thought the person who took them abandoned them. The boy's parents felt the reward was improper. Chic insisted that the boy be rewarded somehow, so he bought a $500 savings bond for him.

By the way, it's way too soon to decide you won't get another dog. Wait awhile. The pain of loss is the price of love. That is way too good to pass over. Death is a part of life. I can't believe I'm saying that, as we buried Wendy yesterday. I know it's risky to compare people to dogs, but I feel so lucky to have had Wendy in my life. To give that up in order to spare pain at her loss is unthinkable. Dogs give us so much joy. They never fail us when even the people we love disappoint us in some way.

What a tremendous person. I wrote her back, "You lost your brother and your niece, and you are comforting me? I am ashamed. You are extraordinary. What a remarkable story."

We had also discussed what I would do to remember Sprite. I wrote, "Kendall and I have decided we will plant a tree on our property when it warms up, and we will place Sprite's ashes around the roots before we cover them with dirt." Debra thought it was a great idea.

Pepsi was showing signs of missing Sprite. They had done everything together—they were as close as any two dogs I'd ever seen. In the mornings, Pepsi would walk through the house, checking each room to see where Sprite was. He seemed to be confused—Sprite was nowhere to be found. Pepsi seemed sluggish at times, not the joyful and playful Pepsi we knew. He was also having nightmares. Pepsi would make short yipping sounds and jerk his body in the middle of the night. He had nightmares before, but these were different.

Sprite's death was felt deeply by Pepsi, so we lavished him with attention and love. The truth is that despite missing Sprite, Pepsi was now having to comfort the human members of his family.

On Monday, four days after Sprite's passing, I called the Montgomery County Humane Society, which had originally rescued Sprite. I wasn't very successful in controlling my emotions when I thanked the person who answered the phone for all their great work. "I don't know how you people do it," I said. "Every day you try to help all these dogs and cats who've lost their families or have been abused. You are angels. And you took care of my Sprite. I just wanted to thank you."

The kind lady answered, "Sir, you are the angel. You adopted him. You cared for him. You loved him."

"I'm no angel," I told her. "I'm just a dog lover who lost a best friend."

But I was becoming more and more guilt-ridden.

Despite all the talk about how wonderful we were to adopt Sprite and care for him, I questioned whether I had, in fact, done all I could to keep Sprite alive. I kept asking myself, Why didn't I have an MRI done when he first collapsed after we adopted him? Maybe some surgical procedure could have been performed. Maybe I could have saved him.

I decided I had to review his medical records. I needed to know for myself whether I had properly cared for Sprite.

I called the Poolesville Veterinary Clinic in Maryland, the first to see Sprite after we adopted him, as they had Sprite's earliest records. Considering the number of animals they had seen during the last two years, I assumed they wouldn't remember Sprite. But the assistant who answered the phone remembered him well. Her name was Patti. I told her I was calling to get a copy of Sprite Levin's records.

"You probably don't remember him," I said.

"Oh, I remember him," she said. "He's white and tan. He's a wonderful dog. And I remember your wife. She's a very nice lady."

I could barely say the words to tell her that Sprite had passed away, but somehow I did. In a downcast voice, Patti said she was sorry. A few days later, Sprite's medical records arrived in the mail.

I also called Chris to retrieve the records from Old Mill Veterinary Hospital, which included the Animal Emergency Hospital file.

I studied all the information.

I looked up medical terms I didn't know.

I carefully matched dates with ailments, appointments, and treatments.

And I came to the conclusion that I had failed Sprite. I failed him because I should have pursued the MRI the first time he had collapsed—that Halloween night in 2004, a few weeks after we had adopted him. I couldn't understand why I had dropped the ball, or worse, why I had decided not to do it. I couldn't remember what I was thinking at the time.

I loved Sprite with all my heart. How could I have neglected him this way?

My depression was getting worse. I couldn't eat. I lost twenty pounds in three weeks. I couldn't sleep.

I asked Chris, "How could I have done this to Sprite?" Chris reviewed all the records and wrote me this note:

Mark,

I have reviewed Sprite's medical record and I know (and you do, too) that you and Kendall did the very best for Sprite. As you know, prior to Sprite's adoption in the fall of 2004, you were unable to know of any previous information about Sprite—whether anything happened or not. You can only make decisions based on the information that you know.

You knew that Sprite had some difficulty getting around when you adopted him. October 31st was the first sign of any neurological problem with his collapse. That problem seemed to resolve and only recurred one other time approximately two weeks later. He never had another collapsing episode. The Poolesville Vet Hosp correctly determined that the problem was not the heart (ECG) and X-rays revealed arthritis and correctly prescribed Rimadyl for the discomfort. I know that you have continuously kicked yourself for not doing an MRI. *It would be very difficult for any veterinarian to strongly encourage the need for the MRI based on the two brief episodes.* Then, a little over one year later, the acute onset of the facial muscles atrophying occurred. Based on a conversation with the local neurologist, he felt the most probable cause was a tumor of that particular nerve (not a brain tumor) that controls that area of the face. An MRI would be the only way to determine this. We decided, based on Sprite's age and not wanting to put him through surgery, that we should try a medication, which was unsuccessful for the face. We just wanted him to be comfortable. Towards the end of this past fall, Sprite started with his pacing through the house, restlessness, etc.

I feel Sprite, who was older than what was initially thought, had multiple issues. He had arthritis that made it difficult to get around. He had weakness in his hind legs that we see in older dogs, which combined with back and hip arthritis severely hampered his ability to move well. I feel that his 2004 collapsing problems were not able to be determined and if it were something that needed to be addressed, there would have been some continuous signs. The facial muscles that atrophied were unrelated to the collapsing episodes.

Chris also explained later that "typically because of the cost, if you do the MRI you need to be willing to pursue treatment (surgery, chemo, radiation, etc.) and in this case treatment most likely included radiation therapy (which includes anesthesia at each treatment)." He added, "I don't think you and

Kendall were ready to put Sprite through the chemo/radiation route."

He was right, and a part of me knows it. But that other part of me will always wonder if there was something more I should have done.

THIRTEEN

The Memory Tree

December 2006–January 2007

Five days after Sprite passed away, Chris came to the house with a small wooden box containing Sprite's ashes. When he handed me the box, I felt as if Sprite had come home. I held it with both hands and couldn't put it down. I had cleared a special place on a shelf in my home office for the box. I eventually placed it there. I decided that when the weather warmed up and the ground softened, I would plant the tree with Sprite's ashes. For the next few days, I'd frequently look at the box. Its contents were precious. But I could not bring myself to open it.

Before he left, Chris said, "Mark, I want you to know something. I see a lot of illness and death in my profession. I am forced to step back from it. But watching you and your family go through this with Sprite, and how much you cared for him, has helped me."

I hadn't thought about it much, but Chris and his colleagues must see terrible cases of abuse or injuries, and they must euthanize scores of animals each year. Veterinarians have to find ways to manage their emotions if they're going to be of any use to their patients and their patients' families. Chris could see my family's pain and my own struggle. He couldn't have been more compassionate. He wanted to help Sprite. He tried to improve and extend his quality of life. Drs. Plant, Bardsley, and Walters used all their training to help Sprite. They all wanted the best for him. It takes uniquely gifted people to work in this profession.

It was time to track down the landscaper I'd talked to earlier about providing us with a tree. He was still working a few houses away. I told him, "My dog has passed away. I want to bury his ashes when I plant the tree. And I don't want the tree to die. It cannot die. I need a tree that can withstand the weather and that won't attract deer. I need a tree that will have blossoms. A beautiful tree."

"I'm sorry about your dog," he said. "I know the feeling. I lost a dog a few years ago."

We talked a little about Sprite and his dog. Then he said, "I have the perfect tree. A Muskogee crape myrtle. It blooms in the summer with lavender-pink flowers. It's about eight feet tall."

"When the weather warms up a bit, I'll need it," I said.

It was now Friday, December 15, eight days since Sprite's passing—the day Lauren was coming home. Kendall picked her up at the airport. We were both going to break the news to her when she got to the house.

For nearly two months, every phone call with Lauren ended with her asking how Sprite was doing, and each time she was told he wasn't great but he'd be okay. Now she'd learn the truth.

During the drive from the airport, Lauren asked Kendall how Sprite was doing. It would be the last time Lauren would have to ask. Kendall had to tell her. It couldn't wait any longer.

Kendall looked at Lauren and said in a soft voice, "Sprite passed away last week, Lauren. I am so sorry."

Lauren started to sob. Then she called me from the car. "Dad, Mom told me about Sprite."

"I'm sorry, Lar. We wanted to tell you sooner, but we couldn't. We wanted to be with you when you heard the news."

Lauren understood. I was so relieved. She knew we kept Sprite's dire condition and then his death from her so she wouldn't grieve by herself.

I felt awful for Lauren. She had a special relationship with Sprite as with Pepsi. When she was home, I often saw her slip the dogs some of her dinner, although I never said anything to her. She would take them for long walks and buy them toys and treats. And Lauren would lie on the family room sofa with Sprite at her side and Pepsi at her feet. Sprite's death would be a hard loss for Lauren. But in the days that followed, she was able to constructively channel her feelings by memorializing Sprite's and Pepsi's lives and time with the family in scrapbooks and photo albums, something for which she has such a talent.

A week had passed since Chris brought me Sprite's ashes. The weather was getting better. Then the day I had waited for arrived. It was sunny and in the low seventies. I had already gone to Home Depot and purchased a pickax, topsoil, and mulch. I had also picked the location for the tree. It was one of Sprite's favorite spots. And it was a good spot. We'd be able to see the tree from the street, the driveway, and the front of the house. I needed to keep an eye on the tree for it would be nurtured by Sprite's ashes. And even though the Sprite I had held and cuddled was gone, in a sense he'd continue to live through this tree.

I had the landscaper drop the tree off that afternoon. He offered to have two of his men dig the hole to plant it. I told him, "I appreciate the offer, but this is something I have to do by myself."

He said, "It won't be easy. The ground is still hard and you need to dig a hole thirty inches wide and twenty inches deep."

"I have to do this," I answered.

My friend Eric was concerned for my health. He worried I might have another heart attack. I told him I'd be fine.

Kendall, Lauren, and Chase were not emotionally up to helping me with Sprite's remains. Besides, the girls were out of town, and Chase was still in school. And I wanted to plant the tree when it had the best chance of taking root and surviving. Today was the day.

Well, the landscaper wasn't kidding. I swung that pickax into what seemed like solid rock for ninety minutes. I had also dragged several heavy loads of dirt, which I had put in my recycling bin as I didn't have a wheelbarrow, to a nearby hill where I dumped them.

I was about 80 percent finished when I came across a telephone line. "Oh great!" I shouted. I had scoped out the area, but not well enough. I hadn't damaged the wire, but I couldn't plant the tree there. So I reclaimed as much of the dirt as I could, dragged it back to the hole, and filled it back in.

At this point I was exhausted. But I couldn't stop now.

I started a second hole right next to the first. This time, it was definitely clear of any wires. Once again, I had to pound away with the pickax. After another sixty minutes, I hit a huge rock. No matter how hard I hit it with that pickax, I couldn't break it. I recalled that my neighbor Andy Fones liked to work in his yard. Maybe he could help.

Andy has a dog named Molly. She's fourteen years old, weighs over eighty pounds, and can barely walk. He carries her outside several times a day to do her business.

I walked down the street to Andy's house and asked him if he had some kind of tool that could remove the rock. He did, and he insisted on removing it for me. Andy could see I was out of steam. And I wasn't about to turn down his offer. He removed the rock in less than five minutes and lugged it away.

The hole was dug. Now came the hard part.

*   *   *

I slowly opened the wooden box that contained Sprite's ashes. They were in a clear plastic bag. I paused briefly, looking at the ashes as I held the bag in my hands. I had put some topsoil at the bottom of the hole. Then I opened the bag with Sprite's ashes and carefully spread them as evenly as I could on top of the soil.

Tears began flowing down my cheeks. It was very tough. I missed him so much. And now he was reduced to a small bag of ashes.

After I emptied the bag, I put the bag back in the box. I put more topsoil over Sprite's ashes. Then I carefully placed the tree in the hole. I shoveled the dirt around the base of the tree and packed it down. With tears still running down my cheeks, I sat next to the tree for a few minutes. I was so tired.

My friend and neighbor Mauricio Mendonca pulled into his driveway. I quickly wiped my eyes, jumped up, and started to open the bag of mulch, but he could tell I was struggling physically and emotionally. "Hey Mark," Mauricio called out. "Would you let me spread the mulch? I'd really like to do it."

Mauricio had been such an important part

of Sprite's life. We were indebted to him and his family for the love they showed Sprite and Pepsi. "By all means," I answered. "I could use the help."

I watched as Mauricio spread the mulch. He then watered the tree and fed it some fertilizer. When he was done, I took a good, long look at the tree. We looked at it together.

It had been less than two weeks since Sprite was gone. Now he was finally laid to rest.

I went inside and put the wooden box in a glass cabinet that hangs on a wall in my office, where it is to this day.

As for the tree, it survived a bitter winter and is doing well. It won't be long before the blossoms appear.

I look at that tree when I wake up in the morning, when I leave the house, and when I return. I cherish it. Apart from my memories, it's all I have left of Sprite.

I often walk up to that tree and say, "How ya doing, Sprite?" And from time to time I touch its leaves and trunk. It seems to help. Sometimes I walk Pepsi over to the tree so he can sniff around and maybe sense his friend's presence.

*   *   *

Kendall decorated the house for Hanukkah and Christmas, as she always does. But it wouldn't be the same. It couldn't be the same. The holidays are an especially difficult time when you're mourning the passing of a loved one. Spritey's stocking was on display with the rest of the family's, but it was empty. Before we opened the gifts, we bowed our heads in silent prayer in memory of Sprite.

It took me six weeks after Sprite's death to get through my depression, although like any dog lover who has lost a best friend, there remain moments of deep sadness.

A few days after his passing, I called my father and mother and asked them how they got through their grief when Lady died. My father said, "Mark, what they say about time healing all wounds is partly correct. The pain becomes manageable, but you never forget." I told them how much I appreciated and loved them.

My parents' mortality is often in my thoughts. I think in some ways Sprite's death is a stark reminder of the inevitable, as was my heart attack and bypass surgery. I identified with Sprite's daily health struggles. It was difficult watching his illnesses eat away at his body. Through it all, he showed us what was important in life. Even at the end, when he could barely stand on his own, he was a bright light who brought sunshine into our lives.

I miss Sprite sitting outside the door, waiting patiently for my radio show to finish.

I miss my late dinners with Sprite and Pepsi.

I miss the unmistakable pitter-patter of Sprite's paws on the hardwood floor.

I miss his bark.

I miss our talks.

I miss our walks.

I miss the wagging of Sprite's bobbed tail and his big smile.

I miss his joy when he greeted us or received a treat.

I miss holding him.

I miss everything about Spritey.

But I also take some comfort in knowing that for the short time he was with us, we doted on him and loved him. He became an indispensable member of our family. He had to know it. I sure hope he did. Sprite touched my heart and opened my soul. I would swear he was an angel.

Sprite's two leashes still hang on the wall in the mudroom, near where we fed Pepsi and him. His medicines remain on a shelf in the pantry. And pictures of the family with Sprite are displayed throughout the house. I put my own photo album together, which I keep on the nightstand. My sweatshirts, which Sprite nested on during his last days, are on a shelf in my bedroom closet.

Every now and then I hold them against my face.

I cannot overstate Pepsi's role in Sprite's life and the life of our family. When I look at our Pepsi, I realize more than ever how blessed we are to have him. I'm so proud of this dog. Another dog might have become jealous or territorial with the addition of a second dog. After all, Pepsi had spent the first six years of his life as an only dog. But Pepsi not only welcomed Sprite into our family, he befriended him. Pepsi was instrumental in making a new and happy home for Sprite. Pepsi is full of life and energy. He's sweet to humans and dogs alike. Pepsi and Sprite quickly grew to love each other. They learned from each other. They picked up each other's traits. They had a rare and beautiful relationship.

Sprite's death was a big blow to Pepsi. He misses his pal. He has his sorrowful moments. But nothing can keep Pepsi down for long. At nine years old, he thinks he's a pup. Yes, he's starting to gray around the snout and eyes, and he rests a little more. He may have lost a step, but it's hard to tell. Pepsi still runs and plays and rummages through the trash can in the kitchen. We've always been very close—from the day I spotted him in the pet shop window. We are even closer now. I have never met a more decent and gentle dog. I don't know what I'd do without him.

Kendall recently said to me, "Sprite's death tore you up. How will you react when Pepsi's time comes?"

"It won't get any easier," I answered.

I dread the day.

While Kendall has shown much strength, her heart bleeds. She found Sprite. She nurtured him through his pain and illnesses. She was always there for him. And Sprite adored her. A few days after Sprite's death, Kendall wrote these words about Sprite:

Sprite came at a time when we had just moved from our home of thirteen years. This was probably one reason we were looking for an addition to the family. I had

left many close friends behind and Sprite's affection was just what the doctor ordered. I now had two doggies following me everywhere I went and who loved me unconditionally. This can be a real blessing when you have hormonal teenagers in the house.

There was something unique about Sprite. He drew people to him like a magnet. He was friendly and fun. I have yet to see another dog who looked like Sprite. Every time we went to the vet I would pore over the dog chart hoping to find a breed that could fit Sprite's look. The closest I found was a Brittany spaniel (which they now have concluded is not a spaniel at all). We always thought he looked more like a small deer.

Sprite was very afraid of a hand coming near his face. We always thought he had been hit often on the snout. Unfortunately, that reflex was so ingrained that it never went away. We would pet him from the back of the head. Yet, when he was offered treats, he immediately sat up and gave us his paw. So somebody had taken the time to teach him. I was so impressed that I finally was able to get Pepsi to do it, also.

Pepsi and Sprite learned so much from each other. They were truly brothers in every sense of the word. And the wonder of it was that it all happened almost immediately. Once Pepsi realized that this dog wasn't just visiting, he accepted him as a member of the family.

Sprite would always circle and circle to find the right position to sleep. We had been told this was nesting. We realized he loved fluffy, comfortable beds and we put them all over the house for him. Pepsi still chose hardwood floors or the carpet.

Sprite and Pepsi were about the same size, but Pepsi had at least ten pounds on Sprite, so he had been too heavy to hold and didn't like being up high on a bed. Sprite was thirty-two pounds and loved being held like a lap dog. He loved cuddling on the bed and stretched out like he was the only one on the bed. When he rested his head on your leg, you knew he was in heaven. Why did we have Sprite in our lives such a short time? Two years just wasn't enough to express all the love we felt for Sprite. He came into our home and immediately fit in. He loved us from day one. This dog, who had been bounced around and experienced who knows what kind of trauma, loved his new life and new family.

But we wondered, did he have a family who was missing him? How could someone with this beautiful, affectionate dog not move heaven and earth to find him? We found him easily on the Internet. Had they looked for him? How long had he been wandering the streets until he was found? Had he gotten lost? As we got to know Sprite and learned of his health problems, we wondered if his original family had known about them. Maybe they couldn't afford a sick dog or didn't want to bother.

Whoever you are, thank you for giving us our two special years with Sprite. He gave us so much more than we could possibly have given him. He pushed himself past the pain to be near us and love us as long as he could.

Thank you, Kendall, for bringing Sprite into our home.

Thank you, Chase, for finding him on the Internet.

And thank you, Lauren, for all those photographs you took of him.

Ten weeks had passed since Sprite's death. One afternoon I got word that the Mendoncas were returning to Brazil that afternoon! Mauricio was staying behind to sell the house and wrap up some loose ends involving his business. But Renata wanted to return to her family, and she needed to leave right away because the kids had to start school in a few days.

Kendall and I thanked the Mendoncas for all they'd done for us. They are extraordinary people who were so loving and caring of Sprite and Pepsi when we were out of town. We will miss them terribly, but never forget them.

I rushed over to their house, which is literally thirty steps away from our house. Mauricio told me that Daniel, who is nine years old, had spent an hour writing a letter to me about Sprite. Daniel handed it to me. When I opened it, I could see all the thought and effort he had put into it. Daniel had printed it in pencil. It said:

The first time I saw Sprite I thought I could make friends with him and his buddy Pepsi. Guess what? It worked out. It was the best day of my life. I saw him almost every single day. One year later something horrible happened. Sprite got a leg and brain disease. I was so sad. A few days later I got to take care of Sprite. We had so much fun. My dad helped, too. Then we took the dogs on a walk. Sprite could not run but Pepsi could. But then something amazing happened. Sprite for the first time ran fast. We played ball. It was so much fun. I wish I could stay forever with Sprite. Sprite was so cute with Pepsi. Sprite had to take a special medicine. What's really cute is that Sprite eats out of Pepsi's bowl and Pepsi eats out of Sprite's bowl. Dad had organized them all the time. If they were good we would give them treats. One of the medicines were eye drops. Sprite would never bite, not even Pepsi.

I gave Daniel a hug and told him, "Daniel, I cannot thank you and your entire family enough. This is beautiful. Sprite and Pepsi love you. And I will always keep this letter."

Sprite and Pepsi enriched so many lives.

FOURTEEN

Griffen

February 2007

It was February. Kendall was up to something. She was leaving the house on the weekends for hours at a time without telling me where she was going. I also found some computer printouts around the kitchen of shelter dogs.

In a stern voice I said, "Kendall, I told you I'm not ready for another dog. We have Pepsi, and that's enough for now."

"Lauren's just looking on the computer," she said.

Then Lauren came over to me and showed me a photograph. "Look at this dog, Dad. Isn't he beautiful? He's blind but he needs help."

"Are you nuts?" I said to her. "Let me be as clear as I can: No new dog!"

A week passed. I was working in my home office. Kendall and Lauren were out somewhere. Chase told me the girls had taken Pepsi for a ride. They were gone for a long time, but I thought nothing of it.

I heard the garage door open. Kendall and Lauren were home. But then I heard a commotion upstairs. Pepsi was making his "devil run" around the house. But I heard something else.

"Oh no, what's that," I shouted. Before I could get up to see what was going on, a small dog came bouncing down the basement stairs to greet me. "Isn't he beautiful?" Kendall said. She had a big smile on her face.

"I told you it's too early for another dog. I can't believe you didn't talk to me about this first."

"If I had told you, you would have said no," she answered.

"That's right, I would have said no. I need another five or six months before we consider getting another dog."

Kendall apologized and said she'd return the dog the next day. She and Lauren had taken Pepsi to a PetSmart in Frederick, Maryland, which was showing dogs that were up for adoption. They had seen a dog sleeping in one of the cages who caught their attention. He had curly fur but they couldn't see his face. They picked him up to see what he looked like. They both looked at each other and knew he was coming home with them. Pepsi and the dog also hit it off. The dog then followed them around the store as if to say, "I'd love to come home with you."

As afternoon turned to night, my apprehensiveness subsided, as Kendall knew it would. I couldn't let her return the dog. God knows what might happen to him if no one else adopted him. It was a fate for which I didn't want any responsibility. As it was, a wonderful group called Friends for Life Animal Rescue Inc. in Monrovia, Maryland, had already saved him from being euthanized by the local shelter, which hadn't been able to find him a family after a few months. Besides, after a few hours with the little guy, I was already attached to him. He was as cute as could be—a mix of poodle and Lhasa apso, they say (I actually think he's part cairn terrier, but what do I know), and he couldn't be more than twenty-five pounds.

I could tell he was happy to be in our home. He explored each room, sniffing here and there. He walked over to each family member, as if introducing himself. He needed and deserved a loving family. My family.

We debated what to name him. Lauren suggested "Dewey" after the drink Mountain Dew. Kendall mentioned "Fresca" or "Fanta." After all, we'd named our other dogs Pepsi and Sprite. Chase and I shot them down. We decided to break from the line of soda names and settled on Griffen.

Once again, Kendall had been told the dog was six years old. And once again I told her, "He's not six years old. He's older." We later learned that he's eleven. As Kendall dug further into his background, she discovered that his owners had decided that their lives were too busy to keep him. They wanted to travel more. So they actually asked their vet whether they should put him up for adoption or have him euthanized! Can you imagine? I have nothing but contempt for such inhumanity and selfishness.

I fired off an e-mail to Chris, asking him to perform a complete exam on Griffen. I wanted to make sure that if there was anything wrong with him, we'd do everything possible for him. Chris responded, "Wow!" He was as stunned as I that Kendall had brought home another dog.

After Chris examined Griffen he told us one of his ears had been severely infected for some time. He said he had to muzzle Griffen to look at his ears because of the pain it caused him. A few months later fifteen(!) of Griffen's teeth had to be removed because they were in such bad shape. And due to persistent problems with his right ear, Griffen recently had a total ear canal ablation—that is, his right ear canal was removed. Had his original owners bothered to care for him, the poor dog would not have had to suffer as he did.

Griffen won't have to fend for himself anymore. He has received excellent medical attention, and from now on he will be properly cared for. It turns out he also has a heart-valve problem. But as someone with his own heart issues, I know there's no reason why he can't live several more years. I sure hope so.

Griffen is now surrounded by people who love him, and a furry friend who will give him companionship. He no longer has to wonder where home is. We're working on his house-training, which means many more early morning and late-night walks. But it's worth it. He's a joy—our little joy.

Moments before Sprite passed away, I looked into his eyes and promised him that we'd never forget him. And I think about him many times every day.

Sprite will never know all the good he did during his short visit on earth and the events he set in motion: Because of him, I was moved to write this book. So it's only fair that a portion of all the proceeds I receive from *Rescuing Sprite* go to dog shelters and rescue groups across the nation, which are overwhelmed with Sprites and Griffens who are in desperate need of food, shelter, medical care, and loving families willing to open their hearts to one of these babies. Rescued dogs, like all dogs, appreciate every kindness.

Nothing will ever replace our beloved Sprite or Pepsi or Griffen.

And in the end, we humans are the lucky ones.

Appendix: The Spirit of Sprite

A few days after Sprite passed away, I received many kind e-mails and cards from friends and listeners. Knowing that others understand what it's like to mourn over the loss of a beloved companion was comforting to me then, as it is today. They may be comforting to you, as well.

Hammer:

I've lived a lot of years and had many a canine friend. My heart has broken with every loss, for they are family in every way.

Upon my return from Vietnam, where I witnessed German shepherds give their lives to save their human comrades, I found my first German shepherd, Duke.

Duke was courageous, loyal, and protective. He was a true part of me. We were inseparable. We ran together. We rode together. We were young together. We could communicate without words. We fought for each other. When he was failing and I was rushing him to the vet, he seemed gone. With the last energy in his being, he rose up and gave me a nuzzle. The eleven years we shared, the best eleven years of my life, were over all too fast, and a part of me died with my beloved friend Duke.

My sympathy goes out to the Levin family. Cherish Pepsi and don't be afraid to add another puppy to your warm family. We are all richer for their love.

With the two shepherds I now have, there have been seven of these loyal companions in my life. With each loss there has been sorrow, with each new pup there has been joy. The joy is much greater than the sorrow. That joy enriches my soul.

In Sprite's memory, let us all honor our companions and reap the joy they can bring.

Flipper:

So I hear that you lost your dog. I'm so sorry. I became so incredibly attached to all my past dogs. To lose a pet, especially a dog, is horrible. More people should respect their dogs and realize how human-like they really are. We just had to put down my golden retriever a year ago. She was fourteen. I had her since she was a puppy. It never gets easier, but she had so much fun and love while she was here. I let her sleep on the bed from day one! Just wanted to send you my condolences. I hope your dog is in doggy heaven with my dogs. We plan on getting one from the pound or North Shore Animal League soon. Your dog is watching over you. I know mine is watching over me. I still dream about her.

Rlusk1:

Mark, my condolences for your loss. I, too, lost both my beloved dogs. Oprah died in 2001 and Whitney in 2004. I could never replace them with any other dogs. I was on a road trip when Oprah died. I was three days away at the time. I regret to this day that I was not there. It happened suddenly without warning. But I know that God sent me a sign that it was okay. I was staying at a cabin with some friends, sitting around a campfire mourning the loss of Oprah. I felt something rub up against my leg and looked down to see a little retriever puppy the same color as my Oprah. The dog looked at me and kinda smiled and then ran off. No one else saw the dog but me. That was God's way of telling me that Oprah was okay with me not being there.

Paul:

Mark, I was saddened to hear you lost your best friend Sprite. I had a little black & white dog my mother adopted which I took after she passed away at only fifty-eight.

Sam lived for another fifteen years until I had to have him put to sleep when he fell prey to brain cancer. I also was the third owner of a sweet German shepherd who hated everyone but me. He was an incredible dog. And his name was Sampson, Sam for short. I had two dogs at the same time named Sam. Not long ago he began having ministrokes, which caused this wonderful dog to collapse to the floor yipping like a baby, unable to stand for minutes at a time. I eventually had him put to sleep to stop his suffering. I promised him I would bury him in the backyard he loved so, where he loved to chase rabbits (never catching any). One night, Thanksgiving eve, I drove my Jeep to a nice corner of my yard, using the headlights to see, and in the pouring chilly rain I tearfully laid my friend to rest along with his blanket and toys. Sam was about nine years old. When I sold my house, I was again saddened when I had to say good-bye [a second time]. This was about six years ago and as I write this, my eyes are filled with tears.

What great loving furry friends dogs are. To this day, I just can't bring myself to get another dog. I was a police officer when I lived in New York and was hurt on the job before I retired on disability, so I was with my guys all the time.

I miss them so much and I know you, too, will miss your best friend forever.

Museum Curator:

Way back on Dec. 7th, 1988, we lost our family dog that I grew up with. To this day, December 7 not only means the day of infamy, it also means the day I lost a good loyal friend. I'm sure for our buddy Mark it will be the same.

My thoughts and prayers go out to the Levin family, Pepsi, and our good buddy Sprite.

Marion:

When you signed off, "Good night, Sprite . . ."

I have dogs. I LOVE my dogs. They're my family. I've enjoyed when you talked about Pepsi and Sprite. Then, the night you told us Sprite's problem . . . and the night you came back in December after being off for about a week . . . I knew then that Sprite was gone, even though you never said a thing until weeks later.

I lost three of my dogs between 11 March 2000 and 11 March 2005 (yes, two I lost on the exact same date five years apart, not by design): two (Shadow and Odin) I'd had since they were puppies, and they had good, relatively long lives; the third (Lady Bug) was a rescue, an older, overweight girl. She wasn't with me even three years when she developed an "overnight" tumor and was gone within four days of its discovery. THAT loss was like being hit in the back of the head by a two-by-four. I still miss the three terribly, still cry at times, still laugh when I think of some of their antics. They've all been cremated. And, when I go, I'll be, too, and have our ashes combined and scattered over trails we loved to hike. Oh, and I keep their ashes in decorative gift bags, and set them under the tree (where they always enjoyed being) at Christmastime.

I just wanted you to know that there are others who share your love and your grief. My thoughts are with you, your pets—both here and gone—and your family.

Acknowledgments

A few days after Sprite passed away, I wrote a short essay about him. Some weeks later I decided to try to turn it into a book. I figured it would not only help me cope with Sprite's death, but possibly help others who were grieving (or will grieve) from the death of their own dog.

I can't count how many times I stopped writing and nearly dropped the project for good. I wondered if anyone would care about what I had to say. I wondered if I was revealing too much about my emotions and family life. And there were times when I thought it would be better to grieve in private. Despite their own mourning, my wife, Kendall, daughter, Lauren, and son, Chase, encouraged me to continue. They're beautiful people and I'm so proud of them. They were active participants in the writing process. This book, like our lives with Sprite, Pepsi, and Griffen, was a family affair.

Throughout my life my wonderful parents, Jack and Norma Levin, have always been a source of wisdom and inspiration. They've always supported my endeavors and been my biggest fans. They are wholly decent and selfless people who've worked hard their entire lives. I am forever indebted to them for all they've taught me, by word and example. They, along with my dear brothers, Doug and Rob, are integral to the book, as they are to my life.

I'm very lucky to have several dear friends who always stand with me and in whom I can confide. Among them is David Limbaugh. David is a superb attorney, columnist, and bestselling author in his own right. He is also my agent. From the start, he had faith not only in my ability to write this book, but that it would be well received by the reading public. I am indebted to him.

Eric Christensen is my vice president at

Landmark Legal Foundation and friend since childhood. On occasion, when I'd go to my office to write late at night, I'd ask Eric to join me so I could bounce thoughts off him. As usual, his advice was top-shelf. Writing this book was emotionally wrenching, as I relived events with my family and dogs while Sprite's death was still fresh in my memory. Eric was compassionate and supportive throughout.

I don't know what I would have done without Dr. Chris Hussion, who helped Sprite and the rest of my family when we most needed it. My friend Chris, Dr. Jessica Plant, Dr. Judy Bardsley, and the team of professionals at Old Mill Veterinary Hospital did everything humanly possible to extend Sprite's life and comfort him in the end. They're truly heroes in my book. Thank you Dr. Norman Walters and his staff at Poolesville Veterinary Clinic, as well as the Montgomery County Humane Society, who took such good care of Sprite in the early days.

Rush Limbaugh and Sean Hannity are two of my closest confidants. They helped me when Sprite passed away and were enthusiastic supporters of this book. I am privileged to be their friend. Debra Burlingame has suffered more hardship than any human being should have to. Yet, she has more faith and strength than I ever will. She was and is an inspiration.

My editor, Mitchell Ivers, is extraordinarily gifted. He has edited many great books by many great authors. He is also a dog lover. And it showed in the outstanding input he provided, which made this a better book. When I first proposed writing a book about my dogs, there were those who doubted I could tell the story, as it seemed to them to be out of character for me. But I knew I could write this book, even though it was different from anything else I had ever written. I had to write it. And Mitchell knew it, as well. I am grateful to him. Mary Matalin, whom I've known and admired for a long time, was a tremendous source of encouragement from her position at Simon & Schuster's Threshold Editions.

My neighbors deserve special thanks. They're too numerous to all be included in the book by name. But I live in a remarkable community, where friends are easy to make and keep. And many of them were involved in Sprite's life in some little way. I will never forget them.

I also want to acknowledge all the fabulous people who are involved in rescuing and caring for abused, unwanted, and lost dogs, who provide financial support to their local dog shelters, and who open their hearts and homes by adopting these wonderful dogs. You have my heartfelt admiration and gratitude. You are very special. God bless you.